Jim Wideman Ministries

BEAT THE CLOCK

SUCCESSFUL STRATEGIES FOR TIME MANAGEMENT

Jim Wideman

D104323P

Unless otherwise indicated, all Scripture quotations are taken from the *King James Version* of the Bible.

Scripture quotations marked (NIV) are taken from *The Holy Bible: New International Version*® NIV ®. Copyright © 1973, 1978,1984 by International Bible Society. Used by permission of Zondervan Publishing House. All rights reserved.

Dictionary definitions are taken from (2009). *Merriam-Webster Online Dictionary.*
Retrieved September 30, 2009, from http://www.merriam-webster.com/dictionary.

Beat The Clock-Successful Strategies For Time Management
By Jim Wideman
Copyright ©2009 by Jim Wideman
Jim Wideman Ministries, Inc.
2441 Q Old Fort Parkway #354
Murfreesboro, TN 37128

ISBN: 978-0-88144-505-3

Published 2009
jim**wideman**.com

Printed in the United States of America. All right reserved under International Copyright Law. Contents and/or cover may not be reproduced in whole or in part in any form without the express written consent of the publisher.

CONTENTS

PREFACE

Time and how you manage it is the difference between whether you are able to accomplish the things that you need to do or not. At the end of the day, it's all about getting what you need to get done, done. One question I'm asked more than any other question is, "How many hours do you work each week?" Before we even start, let's go ahead and answer this question.

As many as I need to! Some weeks I work more than others, but my commitment is to do whatever I need to get everything accomplished for God, my family, and for work. You'll never see your dreams come true when you're just counting hours. A forty-hour workweek is not a biblical concept. It is more important to work smart than to just work harder. It's even better when you do both: work hard and smart at the same time.

In this book you'll learn how to do just that. You'll also learn how to evaluate what you are doing so you can concentrate on accomplishing all that God wants you to accomplish. Time management will help you in every single area of your life from work to play. I believe it's also a habit you can learn, practice, and master. It will help you be a better parent, a better employer, and a better employee; it can help you in every area of your life. So let's get started…

CHAPTER 1

WHERE DID THE TIME GO?

The year was 1993, my itinerary said my destination was the Hillsong conference in Australia, and I was about to embark on the biggest time-wasting day of my life. I left Tulsa, Oklahoma, on Tuesday, arrived in Sydney on Thursday, and I never saw Wednesday. What a waste of time!

But coming home from Australia, I got to experience something I had dreamed about my entire life. Have you ever prayed, "Lord, I wish there were more than twenty-four hours in a day?" Well, don't pray it anymore; it is of the devil. There is a reason why the Lord made a day with twenty-four hours and no more.

Three times now I have had that prayer answered. The first time was in 1993 when I flew home from Sydney, Australia; the second time was when I flew home from Fiji; and the third time was in 2009 coming back from Sydney again. These were all awfully long forty-hour days.

The first time I was traveling back from Australia, I was looking forward to it. Talk about a things-to-do list, I had a things-to-do book. In anticipation of this glorious Monday, I bought extra batteries for my laptop and made up my mind that I wasn't going to go to bed from the time I woke up in Sydney until bedtime in Tulsa. I wanted to see how much I could get accomplished. That long Monday I wrote a personal note to every volunteer we had in our church. I finished reading a book. I got a ton of things done I had been putting off. I wrote several articles and special projects. I really did get a lot done that day.

But, I have to be honest with you. I had the worst Tuesday I have ever had in my life, and Wednesday wasn't a whole lot better. By the time I came out of that coma on Thursday, I realized that God knew exactly what He was doing by putting twenty-four hours, not forty, in one day. And so I never prayed that prayer again. If God's given me twenty-four hours in a day, and that's it, then I need to learn how to manage those hours and not just pray for more to miraculously appear.

Organize and Prioritize_____

There are really only two ways to get more time or be able to get the most out of the time we already have. The first way is to organize and prioritize in order to eliminate time wasters. How much time do we spend every day doing insignificant stuff?

Think about it. When you write a check, do you record how you spent that check in your checkbook register? Do you think that if you just spent, spent, spent; and then sat down once a week, once a day, or once every few hours and tried to remember the amounts and the places where you spent the money, you'd make some slip-ups?

Well, managing your time is a lot like managing your money. We must record how we're spending our time and look at the things that we're doing that are wasteful. When it comes to money, if something on the car breaks and we need money to fix it, we re-evaluate how we're spending our money and begin saying things like, "You know, I cannot eat out for a few days," or "I can do this," or "I change this." When we need money, we look for items in our budget that are not important, and we eliminate those things so that we can use the money elsewhere. It's the same when it comes to your time: record how you spend every minute of the day, evaluate time wasters, and start streamlining your time toward more productive projects.

Use the Time of Others_____

The second way we can get more time is to use the time of others. If somebody else has some extra hours, and you use that somebody's extra hours; then you find somebody else who also has extra hours, and you use that; then you use some more, and some more, and some more . . . Pretty soon you've given yourself access to more than twenty-four hours in one day. I have found that having access to something is really better than owning it.

For example, there is a beautiful house in Newport Beach, California, in an impressive exclusive neighborhood that I could never afford. The house backs up to a bike path, and five minutes away is John Wayne airport. Plus, my family's two favorite malls South Coast Plaza and Fashion Island are nearby. It's such a great place.

This beautiful home is owned by a wonderful woman I know who several years ago said, "Jim, if you and your family are ever in California, I'd love for you to come and stay at my house." For years we didn't take her up on her offer; but when we did, it was the most wonderful gift anyone has ever given us! She went so far as to give me the security code, so we would have direct access into the house. For several years now, my family and I have enjoyed going to Southern California and living like royalty. It's just one of the nicest things that anyone has ever done for us. It is one of the most peaceful and restful places that I go! And, you know, I'd rather have access than own it. If I owned it, I would have to pay for the upkeep and monthly mortgage.

The same principle applies to using the time of other people. When I use other people's extra time, it feels as if my time has multiplied because so much more is getting done; but I don't feel the burden of working those extra hours. And when it's all done, I know that it really is better to have access to something rather than to own it myself.

You Can Be in Control_____

Now, I love my life, I really do. I love all the things that I get to do, but I have a true confession. I have a problem with saying *no*. I am a recovering workaholic. My problem is that I play like I work. I kind of go over the deep end in everything that I do. My wife tells me I have a spiritual gift for taking a good hobby and turning it in to work, so I'm learning that sometimes *no* is just as much the right answer as *yes*.

I love my busy life. I enjoy being in the lives of kids. I enjoy all the things that I get to do at World Outreach Church. Right now I oversee everything from birth through college. At my former church I also had the opportunity to oversee lots of areas for different seasons, and when someone on staff left our team, I got to oversee that area until we hired the right person. God has called me to ministry and the many facets it entails, but that does not mean I do not have to steward my time. I am still responsible for controlling what I do and do not do.

If you are not in control of the way you spend your time, it will overtake you. You will not live long enough on this earth to accomplish everything God has called you to. There is a difference between being busy and doing the right thing. You must always stay in control of your time.

Just Because You're Willing_____

> *Now you are the body of Christ, and each one*
> *of you is a part of it.*
>
> 1 Corinthians 12:27 NIV

I believe with all my heart that this verse is true and applies to time management. We are all the body of Christ and members in particular. Do you know that you can get in a lot of trouble if you are a finger and you try to be a nose; or if you're a nose and you try to be an ear?

So many ministries I know, especially when it comes to placing volunteers, are like Frankenstein. They've got parts in the wrong places. Because someone was willing to work in one area of ministry, they put that person there. Even if that person didn't have the abilities, gifts, or skill set needed to do the job, they used them simply because that person was willing.

When it comes to managing your time, just because you are willing to do something does not mean it is the best use of your time. Willingness is not the standard for whether or not you should take on another commitment. I have found in my own life that I have been drawn in to time commitments because I was willing. But if I'd stopped, prayed, and really looked at it, or if I had even talked to my wife about it, I may have realized it was not the best use of my time. So when you look at ways to manage your time, be sure you are focusing on areas where your gift and calling has made room for you. Take your proper place in the body, and allow others to do what they are called to do. Everybody is a different part of the body, and when we all work in our proper places, God can move in great ways.

Good Choices Versus *God* Choices_____

Since we are living in the last days, it's important that we examine our lives to make sure we are ready for when Jesus returns. Look at Ephesians 5:15-17 NIV:

Be very careful, then, how you live—not as unwise but as wise, making the most of every opportunity, because the days are evil. Therefore, do not be foolish, but understand what the Lord's will is.

Do you believe that Jesus is coming back soon? If so, the Bible has instructed you to "make the most of every opportunity." Time management helps you do just that. When you manage your time, you can identify what's important, what's not important, how you can spend your time more wisely, and the things you need to eliminate that are taking away your focus. There are always a lot of good things that you can do with your time, but they may not be what God has really ordained and *called* you to do.

The devil understands that if he can get you to chase *good* ideas rather than *God* ideas, then He can keep you running circles, and you will never accomplish the plan God has for your life. This is why it's so important to evaluate how you spend your time. Time is short, and Jesus is coming back. Don't get into the rut of filling your schedule with *good* choices when you can be focusing your time on *God* choices.

It's important to be careful how you live and to look at how you spend your time. Manage and do those things that you are the best at doing. I know there are a lot of things you *can* do, but *should* you? That's a question that I have to deal with in my own life. Today, as you're reading this, I know that when I'm pointing at you, there's three more fingers pointing back at me.

Time Is Important to God_____

There are all kinds of Scriptures that point out that how we spend our time is important to God. In fact, the word *time* is used over 700 times in the Bible. One verse that discusses how we spend our time is found in Ecclesiastes 3:1 NIV. It says, "There is a time for everything, and a season for every activity under heaven."

In Genesis 1 we see that God had an agenda for each day in the story of creation. Have you ever wondered why He didn't just do it all in one day and goof off the rest of the time? I've often wondered that. But what was He showing us? He was showing us that He had an agenda. Every single day of creation God had a to-do list. There's a principle there. When you follow God's example and make a to-do list, you get to do something that a lot of us miss; you get to take a day off. God was able to rest; He was able to relax. He was able to, again, set an example for how we are to how spend our time. You see, this idea of a to-do list and an agenda is a biblical concept.

Romans 14:12 NIV talks about the judgment seat of Christ, but I also think it goes along with time management. It says, "So then, each of us will give an account of himself to God." Now, how can you give an account of yourself if you don't know how you're spending your time? It's important that we realize that it's not just about looking at how we want to spend our time; it's analyzing how we want to spend our time, how we should be spending our time, and how we've actually spent our time that's going to cause us to do great things. The happiest people I know are the people that understand and spend their time according to the plan God has for their lives, rather than allowing days, weeks, months, and even years to go unaccounted for.

Now, when we watch how we spend our time, we're able to accomplish more for God with the time He's given us. And isn't that the bottom line—to accomplish what God has put us on this earth to do? There's a phrase that every single one of you want to hear when you stand before the Lord, "Well done, my good servant…. Because you have been trustworthy in a very small matter, take charge of ten cities" (Luke 19:17 NIV). We must be faithful with what God has called us to do because that's where promotion and increase come from. That's where the blessing of hearing "well done" will happen. You see, I like my steaks rare, but I want my works to be well done.

CHAPTER

2

BUSY IS A RELATIVE TERM

Here's a dumb question. (I always say there's no such thing as a dumb question, but my definition of a *dumb question* is a question you already know the answer to.) Would you consider yourself to be busy? I figured as much.

But I've found over the last thirty years of working in churches that *busy* is a relative term. When I have thought that it could not get any more hectic, any busier, it did. On the other hand, the times I thought were busy were actually slow.

Let me tell you a little bit about my story. In 1990, I moved to Tulsa, Oklahoma, to work for a ministry where I could train children's workers and other ministry leaders. My girls grew up watching video programs that this ministry put out to churches across America, so they were just as excited as we were to move. When I came on staff, it was right before the third birthday of the church; the pastor didn't really want to be gone much from the church; so he'd start off the regional conferences, and I'd end them. Plus, I taught a lot of the sessions in between. At the end of each conference, I came back on cheap Sunday airfare. And that's how I started. Also, the ministry was about to start a Bible college to train children's and youth pastors. Since I was one of the only children's pastors he knew who had a college degree, I got drafted to head up the school as well.

I'll be honest with you. One of the most exciting aspects of this job was that I would be working with children's workers and teaching about children's ministry; but I didn't have to recruit anybody. I didn't have to handle budgets, or the lack thereof. I didn't have to handle some of the problems of a growing church. I got to do ministry, have a job, and preach to adults; yet I didn't have to deal with the problems of children's ministry.

That was in June. Well, July came along, and the pastor (and most of his staff) went on vacation. So I asked them, "What do you want me to do while I'm here?" because at the time I was primarily doing road stuff and didn't spend much time ministering at the church. He instructed me to look at all the church's ministries, note what was happening, and give a report when he returned.

Well, being a classically Southern-Baptist trained Christian education guy (and a workaholic), I went overboard on my report. I looked at all of our different children's and youth ministries and noted the goals we were not accomplishing. There were just all kinds of obvious things that I saw us doing, or not doing, that we needed to change in order to be a true role model to the churches we ministered to. At the time, we weren't even using the curriculum our pastor had written and published. After all the evaluating, I worked with my team to come up with a plan to fix and solve our various weaknesses.

When my pastor returned, I gave him my report; and he asked, "Can you do this?"

"What?" I asked.

"Can you do the stuff that's on here?"

"Yes," I answered, "that's what I've done at my other churches." All of the sudden, besides doing the road stuff and the crusade stuff and working on the school of ministry, I also became the Christian Education director and was put in charge of the youth pastor and the children's pastor.

A few years down the road, as things rocked on, we started growing different ministries, doing different things, and even taping video shows where I was not only on the writing staff, but also cast as the barber of the town. So I was working at the church, traveling, writing a preschool show, and acting in movies and videos when the time came to start the school of ministry. My pastor told me that I didn't have time to be the head of the school of ministry and do all the things that I was presently doing to help him. But that didn't mean I was any less busy. In fact, I was elected to teach ten classes at the school of ministry. So, what did that do to my schedule? Tuesday through Friday mornings I taught ten classes and none of my other responsibilities were dropped. Because of teaching, I had half of the time to get it all done, so that meant I had to do all the rest of my work in the afternoon.

It was the best thing that ever happened to me because it made me look at things that only I should be doing and identify the things I was doing that others could do. I'm still realizing things others can do to free me up to do what I need to be doing.

Is there such a thing as being "too busy"? Yes, I think you can be. But a lot of times, what people think is "too busy" is just "busy." The reason they're not getting things done is because of bad time management. Now, you can't manage everything: it doesn't make sense for one person to try to do the work of three or four people. I've tried it, and it just doesn't work out. But at the same time, being busy is not bad. It's being busy and not accomplishing what you need to that's bad.

We Make Time for What We Want_____

Busy is a relative term. You can always get busier. No matter how busy you are, life can get crazier. But I've also found that no matter how busy it is, I always have time to do the things that I really want to.

For me, it's guitars. I'm one of those guitar players that have been playing long enough that all of my toys have become antiques. The first electric guitar I bought was a 1964 baby blue Fender™ Mustang. When Kurt Cobain died, I watched this thing go from 475 dollars on the vintage market to 1,200 dollars just because some freak, who used to play one, killed himself. And that got me going with the hobby of just kind of looking at the values of those things. You know, I can be really busy, but if somebody calls me about his or her granddaddy's guitar and says, "Man, my granddaddy has a 1932 Martin™. Do you know how much it's worth?" I have time to find out. Because I'm interested in that, I'll take time to go look in a book and tell that person,

"Hey, that thing's worth $25,000 right now. You know, I'd have to see the condition and some different things, so bring it by Wednesday night, and let me drool over it on your way to church."

I also love my daughters. And I realize that if I reach every kid in America and my own two girls don't have a relationship with daddy, I have my priorities messed up. I still have dates with my daughters. My oldest daughter is married, and I still have dates with her and my youngest daughter every week. It's just a standing thing that we have. Whoever can come, comes. If daddy has to kick it in the head, or if they have to kick it in the head, that's fine; but we have a standing date that basically started when they were both weaned. I always have time for my girls because I have learned that you make time for the things you want to make time for. The key is to want to do the right stuff—the things that God wants you to do.

3

TIME MANAGEMENT

It's Like Driving a Car_____

Could you drive a car the day you were born? No? But you learned how to do that. How about feeding yourself? No, but you learned. (I learned that very well.)

I have a true confession for you. I was not born organized. A lot of people think that people are either born organized or born without the ability to organize. Listen, we all came into this world the same way—naked. If Mama hadn't been at the hospital, we would've been in a lot of trouble. Thank God she was there.

Organization and time management are learned behaviors. And while there are certain things you learn better than others, when you learn how to manage things, you really will get better at doing them. It's like anything else; practice makes perfect. The more time you spend honing a skill, the better you are.

One time, the musician Lincoln Brewster came to minister at the church I was working at, and somebody made an observation that I thought was really good. He began, "Boy, I bet he had a sorry childhood."

"You think he had a sorry childhood?" I asked.

And the guy said, "Yeah, he never played outside. He just practiced his guitar. That guy's fabulous."

"I'd never thought about it like that," I said

"But, you know," he continued, "He must not have had any friends and must not have played any ball because he was just stinking awesome."

That guy understood that you don't get that good without practice. You develop and hone your skills, even time management skills, by spending time working, developing, and practicing them. Just like you can learn leadership principles, you can learn to be a better time manager.

I'll be honest with you; I used to not know anything about time management. When I was younger, I was close to flunking out of school. Sure, I was having a great time, and I was very popular on campus, but my grades were suffering because I didn't know how to manage my time.

One day I had a professor pull me aside and say, "Jim, you're a smart guy, but you need to get some organizational skills working in your life." So he showed me how to write assignments and their due dates down. Then he showed me how to think in steps: if I needed to write a term paper, the first step was to go to the library. If I didn't do that first step, just because I had put the due date on the calendar did not guarantee it would get done

Santa Knows Best_____

Make a list and check it twice. I call that fat-boy organization. I'm not the only fat bearded guy that does that: I learned it from Santa Claus. Organization is making a list and checking it and then walking it out in organized steps.

Some people think organization is a systematic way of doing things. Others might define it as just getting things done. Let's look at what Mr. Webster says, "the act or process of arranging by systematic planning and unified effort." I define it as the vehicle that causes me to get everything done in my life and be ready for more.

I've found that in organization there is a good way to handle your responsibilities, and there is a better way. Sometimes you can be so busy with different jobs that if God was to bless the main job that you have, you couldn't handle the increase. So the key is not just to manage what you're doing now, but organize your time in such a way that you are also able to manage increase. Don't take on extra things that God doesn't lead you to because they will consume your life with unnecessary busyness, and then you will not be able to manage the increase that God brings your way.

If organization is a "systematic planning and unified effort," then there must be a formula. There is. It's simple:

$$\text{ORDER} + \text{ORGANIZATION} = \text{MANAGEMENT}$$

Order

Order is arranging things by priority or importance. We know order was established by God because heaven is an orderly place. Job 25:2 NIV says, "Dominion and awe belong to God; he establishes order in the heights of heaven." It's important we see that our job in ministry, as well as in our personal time, is to look at things and give order to them. The Bible tells us that all things should be done decently and in order.

A few years ago, one of my girls, who is usually pretty happy, was acting pretty sad. Since that was kind of weird for her, I sat down and tried to help her figure out what the problem was. I asked her, "Alright, tell me your priorities. What are the most important things in your life?" We wrote down what she said, and then I had her write down how she was spending her time.

When we had finished and she compared the two, she looked at me and said, "Dad, my priorities are mixed up."

I encouraged her, "Yeah, baby. Now, anytime you need daddy to help you with this exercise, I'll help you. But the smart thing is for you to look at your priorities and how you're spending your time, and keep those things in order."

The Bible says a man of understanding and knowledge maintains order, and I want to be that kind of guy. So over the years, in both my household and my life, I have had to look and see if I had something out of order and fix it so that I could maintain order in my life.

My favorite Scripture in the entire Bible is found in Proverbs 28:2 NIV, "When a country is rebellious, it has many rulers, but a man of understanding and knowledge maintains order." I've found this true in my personal life, in my kids' lives, in my family life, and in my ministry. Whenever there's something wrong, there's usually something that's out of order that needs to be examined, tweaked, and looked at.

Organization

Organization should be a natural part of life. It's a process. The key to thinking organized, is to think systematically. In other words, come up with a simple process to do the things that need to be done routinely. If you find yourself needing to do something on a regular basis, come up with a system. Systems just naturally get complicated, so that's why you have to be intentional about keeping things simple.

Without organization and order, you won't have things in place that you need to be able to benefit you. Have you ever noticed that when you clean out a closet to get things in order, sometimes you have to make a mess before the thing is straightened out? Halfway through, all you see is a big mess, and you might think, *Man, I spent the whole day doing this, and I didn't really accomplish that much.* But when you put it all back where it can be useful and help you, all of the sudden that organization and new system allows you to manage things better.

My wife was telling me she watched this show the other day on TV about a family that has nineteen kids. One of the most amazing segments was about this ten-year-old boy who was in charge of the family's pantry. He stood on a ladder telling everybody things like, "Sugar goes over here. Flour goes over there." He had a place for everything in that cupboard. (I know some people that need to hire him as a warehouse manager.) This young man was getting some valuable organization training, and he was only ten!

Management_____

Management is the key to promotion. Going back to the "well done" story, let's look at the Bible in Matthew 25:14-23 NIV. In verse twenty-three, the servant's master replies, "Well done, good and faithful servant! You have been faithful with a few things; I will put you in charge of many things. Come and share your master's happiness!" Because this servant was faithful, he was promoted. What caused him to do that? Management—the combination of order and organization.

Again, managing small things well is an indicator of how you'll handle more. Listen, the more things you can do well, the more valuable you are to any organization. Just don't do anything and everything. Manage the things you *should* be doing well, and then you will be more valuable.

Years ago, I had a lady come to me and say that she would come to my church if I made her the preschool director because she liked running things.

I responded, "Well, you don't need to come to our church unless God's called you to come to our church. I'm not going to give you a position just so you will come to our church because that's not how God promotes." She got mad and didn't join our church, but I knew that there was no way I could promote somebody that I didn't even know. Plus, I could not rely on someone who was only committed to our church because she was in charge of something. The only way to tell if she was going to be faithful in running something would have been to put her over something small and see how she did. That's the biblical way of doing things because the Bible tells us that if we are faithful in small things, we will be rulers over much.

One phenomenon that has blown me away over the years is how God has always provided experienced children's workers to work under me at each church I've worked for. Some were children's pastors at other churches before they moved to come and help me. Some of these folks were very gifted and talented, and they did a wonderful job working for me. But, you know, they didn't start off that way. They started off doing the exact same thing that any person with no experience would do—they were faithful with the small stuff. If you're not faithful in small things, then there's no indicator as to how you'll do with the big things.

In 1979, I had been working for about a year in my first church. I was all excited about our children's ministry and what we were doing, not just in our city but also in our state. We were able to minister to more than just our church people through our affiliation with the Assemblies of God. At that time, the district CE director called me and asked if I would help on their Sunday school tour. Basically, I'd be part of a team going throughout the district holding conferences and seminars. I accepted readily, so he promised to call me back with details.

He didn't mention anything about teaching or preaching, but I, at the time being the only paid children's pastor in the state of Mississippi, thought, *You know if we're doing something on children's ministry, I'll probably get to teach it.* I was so excited. It was my first opportunity to teach someone other than the people in my church. I even told my pastor, "Man, I think I'm going to get to help with the Sunday school tour." He was excited for me too.

Then, a few days later, the director called back and asked if I still wanted to help. I reassured him that I was eager to help, and he proceeded to explain that he needed me to be in charge of refreshments. Boy, my heart sank. I asked if he needed me to teach anything, but he said that all of the pastors would take care of that.

My heart was broken, but you know what? When I prayed, the Lord said, "This is an opportunity to do something well. It might be small, but you need to do it well."

Right then I decided and prayed, "Lord, I want to handle the job of refreshments like I would handle the job of a keynote speaker."

As the time for the Sunday school tour drew closer, I started researching and planning. I did my homework to locate local bakeries and restaurants around the state. When it was show time, I had put together a spread that only a fat guy could do. I mean it was just something for everybody.

But I didn't stop planning once the first meeting was through. I was so excited about those refreshments that I kept looking for ways to tweak my presentation. I'd set up little meetings with some of the women and show them a picture of my food table and ask, "How can we make this better? Can we add some food art?" The next time we presented we added a watermelon basket.

You see, rather than getting my feelings hurt and having a pity party because nobody wanted to hear me preach, I realized I had an opportunity to have a ministry; it was just a different type of ministry—a ministry of donuts. And each time we had another service, I looked for ways to improve, tweak, and make a plan so that the next presentation would be even better.

My diligence paid off. The director even came and told me that each conference's refreshments were better than the one before. Not only that, but I'll never forget a pastor's wife in Oxford, Mississippi, who paid me the highest compliment. She was standing there with a butter cookie on one finger and a donut on the other, and she said, "Who was over the refreshments? They need to do this all the time."

The Sunday school tour was every other year, so two years later when they did it again, the director called me and asked for my help. When I asked if I was over refreshments again, he told me that this time he needed me to teach. If the first time he asked for my help, I had had a bad attitude and said, "Well, if I can't teach, I'm gonna do nothing," I would not have been promoted to do what my heart's desire was. It's so important to take care of the small things because that will always indicate how you'll do with big things.

Neglect Is Loss_____

Being a bad manager is the same thing as being irresponsible. God doesn't want us to be irresponsible with the things that He has given us. So, how do we keep from being irresponsible? We learn how to manage well.

Whatever you do not manage, you lose. This is true with money, with ministry, with family, with relationships, and it's also true with your time. All of these are important, but wouldn't it be nice to be able to decide that you're only going to manage one of them? The problem is when you look at every activity in your life, all of these categories are involved. We all have to learn how to manage or else one or more of these areas is going to lose out. It may sound overwhelming, but you can learn how to manage them all at the same time.

Growth Is Good_____

I want to make this clear right now. There is nothing wrong with being in a small church, but the New Testament pattern for churches is to grow. Every time I see my mom, she thanks her God that I was born small. She is so glad she did not give birth to me full grown. It is not God's plan to give birth to full-grown babies, literally, nor in the form of something like a church.

Everything starts small. That is a biblical principle. But if it stays small, it's time to do a little check-up. Take it to a specialist, see what in the world is going on, ask some questions, tweak some things, and make some changes. Why? So growth can happen.

The sad thing is, there are a lot of churches that aren't doing that. They've accepted the fact that since they were born that size, they're going to stay that way. They reason that since they've been a church of fifty people for the last fifty years, why change now?

"Oh, Brother Jim, we don't live in the book of Numbers. We live in the book of Acts."

Well, read Acts. It's full of numbers! And every time there was a number in the book of Acts, it got larger. Start at chapter one, and look at the numbers. The numbers increase. That's God's plan. The Bible says to add to the church daily. That means every church ought to grow at least 365 people a year.

While I'm in this neighborhood, let me say that I'm glad when Christians come to our church, but there is a difference in population shift and new birth. And God hasn't just called us to have a big crowd; He's called us to go into the world and make disciples. It's important that we understand this.

4

KEYS TO ORGANIZATION

One-Dimensional Is Not an Option_____

Too many leaders I know in leadership positions are one-dimensional people. They just can't handle multiple things at one time. The problem is that life is multi-dimensional. And to master a multi-dimensional life, you must learn how to think multi-dimensionally and learn to multitask. Multitasking is working with multiple assigned pieces of work that all need to be finished within a similar timeframe.

When I was in college, I felt like every professor thought that their class was the only one that I was taking. Everything was due at the same time. I thought they were just being cruel and didn't like me. It was really frustrating, but I had no earthly idea they were preparing me for life. It turns out that those teachers were my friends because that's the way life is: it's multiple assigned pieces of work that have to be done at the same time. If you don't learn how to multitask, you're not going to be promoted.

Now, here's the thing. The not doing them isn't necessarily a problem. Most of the time we're able to get them done. It's the doing them all *well* that seems to cause the most issues.

So where do you start? As I said before, ORDER + ORGANIZATION = MANAGEMENT. It all starts with order and organization.

Six Basic Keys to Organization_____

1. Get a vision.

The first thing you need is a vision. Stephen R. Covey says in his book *Seven Habits of Highly Effective People* that the number-one habit is to start with the end in mind. If you've ever taken a trip to a city you've never been to, you know you have to start by taking out a map and locating your destination. You may have thought your destination was close to another city you've been to before, but if you had tried driving to that city, you would've soon figured out you were on the wrong side of the state. Even if you call a travel agency before you leave and say, "I want a map"; they're still going to ask,

"Where are you going?" They could just hand you a map, but that's not necessarily going to get you to your desired destination.

You've always got to know where you're going. That's all a vision is—where you want to end up. Discovering God's vision and what He has called you to be follows the same principle. You must see it before it comes to pass. If you're going to get organized, you've got to know where you're headed. You've got to see it before it happens.

Years ago I ran in to someone I knew during a meeting we were doing in Florida, and she said, "Oh, Brother Jim, I've heard about how your church has grown in Tulsa. And I heard about all the things you're getting to do and how you're getting to travel!" Then she asked, "Did you ever in your wildest dreams think you'd be doing that?"

I had to be honest with her, "Yes, in fact, I wondered what took Jesus so long because I saw the vision long before it happened."

You see, the vision to go in to children's ministry came in an unconventional way. I was not called into children's ministry; I was drafted. While I was working at a church in Jackson, Mississippi, the lady that was leading the children's ministry quit, so my pastor told me to take my Bible and my guitar, go to children's church, and not to come out. I did exactly that. As soon as I got there, I started praying, "Oh, God, oh, God, give somebody a vision for children's ministry. Open their eyes, Lord. Let them see the value of kids. Oh, Lord, it's not babysitting. It's ministry. Show them." And after praying that prayer and working with the kids over the next few weeks, I realized I was the person He'd given the vision to, because I was seeing children's ministry through Jesus' eyes.

Once I had accepted that God was calling me to children's ministry, I decided the first thing I would do for the kids was take them to kids' camp. So that summer I loaded the kids on a bus and headed to Uporia, Mississippi, to a Church of God prophecy camp. Here I was, just packed to the gills with kids in this bus, heading to a facility we rented. The end of the world isn't in Uporia, Mississippi, but you can see it from there. The old camp was even rougher. It had this old egg water, and the kids would actually take Sprite™ and brush their teeth with it because it was better than the water.

During chapel, I remember the evangelist saying, "Everybody come down to the altar." You know, it was one of those things where they were going to get everybody at the altar one way or the other, so everyone might as well go down, get on their faces, and suck rug. Otherwise, the service would go all night until everyone did.

While I was kneeling around the altar with the kids, I remember praying, "Lord, I want to do more for You. I thank You for allowing me to work with kids, but show me, show me, Lord, Your plan."

In a moment, bigger than life, I saw myself preaching before more kids than I've ever seen before. I saw opportunities and ministries God would have me lead, and it just blew me away. That night, the Lord gave me a vision of what I could accomplish in children's ministry, so I went back to my cabin, wrote down that vision, and began to make a plan.

It took ten years for everything in that vision to pass—ten years and three churches. I made a lot of mistakes, did a lot of stupid things, but God kept His promise. As God opened doors for each part of that vision to happen in my life, I'd check them off my list. When I checked off the last thing on that vision, I remember looking back at how I'd grown and how many things God added to my life, and I prayed, "Lord, I'm at the end of this vision. Either increase this vision, give me a new one, or take me home, because I refuse to live on this earth without a vision."

It was at that particular time that God called me to Tulsa. And for seventeen years, I was a part of one of the biggest visions that I have ever seen in my life. Whenever my pastor came to me and said the three most dreaded words, "I've been thinking," I knew I was getting ready to get after it, to do something big, to do something well.

Vision is the key to moving forward to better things in life. I am a better person because of vision in my life. In fact, I've gotten to the point that I can honestly say, "I don't have a big vision. A big vision has me." That's important.

Vision isn't just for the grown-ups. I've learned in parenting that the best thing I can do for my kids is to help them get a vision too. When Yancy, my oldest daughter, was little, God started showing her that she would write songs and be a musician. I never had to tell her to practice. The vision dictated that she practice. Kids that know God has called them to be a doctor don't have to be told to study. The vision dictates that they study.

Now, I don't think every child at a young age can know exactly what God wants him or her to do, but parents can certainly start pointing their kids in the direction of their interests, likes, and the things they naturally do well. If God's in that, He'll use it. He'll help them to the next step and the next. Again, it's a vision that helps us to become organized and do these things.

Proverbs 29:18 KJV says, "Where there is no vision, the people perish." Let's put it another way. Where there is vision, people flourish. The best thing that I could encourage you on your journey to becoming organized, is to start with finding your vision. Pray, "Lord, where do you want me to end up? What do you have planned for my life? My family? My job? My church? Show me Your vision."

2. Write Your Goals in Steps

If you're going to be organized, besides having a vision, you need to have goals in order to accomplish everything. Philippians 3:14 NIV says, "I press on toward the goal to win the prize for which God has called me heavenward in Christ Jesus." I like to say it this way: If you aim at nothing, you hit it every time. There are lots of leaders who aren't hitting anything right now.

I'm a goal-oriented person, and I've learned that sometimes handling the big goal just won't get you through. Most people can't handle the big picture. You have to break things down into smaller goals to be able to hit the big goal.

For example, if you have a goal of losing one hundred pounds, you can't just decide that you're going to lose one hundred in a week. It will probably make you extremely sick. The only way I know you can lose one hundred pounds is to break that down into short-term goals.

When my youngest daughter, who's twenty-five, was a preschooler, we moved out to Tulsa. She was a member of a Christian video club, and she used to tell time by how many videos it was until somebody came over. So, if we were having dinner guests, she'd ask, "Daddy, how many shows until Mr. and Mrs. So-and-So come over?"

So I'd tell her, "Three shows." She knew that after a whole video and half of another one, our guests would arrive.

When we made the big move from Alabama to Oklahoma, she came to me and said, "Daddy, how many shows until our new house in Oklahoma?"

Now, I knew if I told her it would take forty-six shows that was too much for her preschool mind to handle. So, we broke the trip up in to multiple destinations. First, we went to grandma's house in Birmingham, and then we went to the state line. From there we went to Memphis, and after that, we spent the rest of the day in Arkansas.

I'll never forget when we jumped out of the car at the McDonald's on the Muskogee Turnpike, Whitney asked, "Daddy, how many shows till our new home?"

I smiled and told her, "Baby, just two shows, and we'll be there."

"One video, and we're there? Just one video?" Oh, she was excited. Why? Because we had broken the trip up into small goals that even a preschooler could handle.

That's the same way with getting organized. Don't look at Z and pray, "Lord, I want Z!" when He's given you A, and you haven't even finished that. Why do you need Z? Z is irrelevant. You don't even need Z to do A. Stop praying, "I want Z, Lord!" Do A, and then He'll give you B. Do B, and He might let you skip to D. But take those steps.

You've got to think in steps. When I was working at a church in Oklahoma, we reorganized and revamped our children's ministry at least three dozen times in the seventeen years I worked there. Some people think that we just organized our church one time and the thing grew, but there were multiple times that I would go into every classroom and look at every detail and tweak and make changes. Sometimes, I completely changed what we were doing. But it didn't all happen overnight. It took small steps from one good procedure to the next for the children's ministry to grow.

Psalms 37:23 says, "The steps of a good man are ordered by the Lord: and he delighteth in his way." Notice David says, "the steps"; it doesn't say "the leaps" or "the jumps" of a good man. That's why you must write down your goals in steps.

3. Prioritize

You must live by priorities. Everybody says that they have priorities, but that doesn't mean they live by them. And just because you can tell people what your priorities are, doesn't mean you're living by them. You must establish order in your goals and do what is the most important. Conversely, if you don't have priorities, you cannot keep them.

In order to begin establishing your priorities, you must first figure out what are the most important things in your life. I believe that everyone who is a Christian will say that first and foremost is a relationship with Jesus Christ.

According to the Word of God, my number-two priority is my family. I don't know if you have noticed this, but God created the home before the church or any other institution. And no matter what your family priorities may have been until now, the biblical order is your spouse first and then your kids.

You know, your kids won't always live at your house, but you'll always be a parent. I'm on a different parenting trail right now than I've ever been on before. Right now we only have one at home. She mainly just changes clothes and then she's off to her various jobs and social engagements. Regardless, I know I'll see her at our weekly daddy/daughter date, but that's about it. My oldest daughter is married to a cute husband, (so I know I'm going to have the best-looking grandkids), and they have their own house. Because my girls are grown, I don't see either of them as much, and if I didn't have a relationship with my wife, I might be freaking out over the empty nest thing. But I'll be honest with you, I enjoy being with just my wife. I did not marry the mother of my children; I married the girl of my dreams. She is still the girl of my dreams. And because I kept her the priority over my girls, the transition in to being the parent of adult children is much smoother.

After your relationship with Christ and your family, a newer priority I've had to give attention to is health and exercise. Listen to me. If you die, you cannot accomplish what God has put you on this earth to do. If I die, I can't be the one that gives my youngest daughter away at her wedding. Also, I want to watch my future grandchildren grow up, and I can't do that unless I make my health a priority.

I started riding my bicycle as a form of exercise and fun. Soon a group of fellow cyclists from my church began riding with me on a consistent basis, and the first time I rode in an organized long-distance ride, over fifty people from my church rode too. In 2005, I rode an average of 2,000 miles from time change to time change. Plus, I got to ride in my first century (one-hundred-mile bike ride). It was really my second century, but during the first one, on mile seventy-five on the Pacific Coast highway, I hit a car and did $3,500 worth of damage to an Infinity™ with my knee. It wasn't fun, but it made a good story. From all the time cycling, I learned that I could make exercise a priority and not sacrifice fun and social time in the process.

Next on my list of priorities are my pastor's (boss's) problems. I have no other problems than my pastor's problems. When my boss wants to see me, I go talk to him, find out what his problems are, and find out what I can do to help.

My fifth priority is the level of leadership directly under me. Where'd I learn that? Jesus. He had a public ministry, but He was never too busy for Peter's dumb questions. Not one time in the Bible after a day of Jesus talking to thousands of people (without a microphone), did He ever ignore his disciples' questions. Not one time is it recorded that he told them, "Oh shutest thou upeth," or "Oh get away from me, thou dumb idiot."

Listen. Ministry is hard now—and that's with air-conditioning and PA systems. Can you imagine what Jesus felt like? He was God, but He was man. And, you know, those sandals didn't have a lot of support, yet He walked almost everywhere. Think about it: He talked all day, and He still had time to answer His followers' questions. In fact, there's more recorded of what He told His disciples than what He said publically. He spent a lot of time with His workers—maybe that's why He was able to accomplish in three years what takes us eons. He saw the importance of spending time with the level of leadership directly under Him.

Look at Matthew 12:47-49 NIV:

"Someone told him, 'Your mother and brothers are standing outside, wanting to speak to you.'

He replied to them, 'Who is my mother, and who are my brothers?'"

That sounds kind of cold, doesn't it? But then He pointed to His disciples and said, "'Here are my mother and my brothers. For whoever does the will of my Father in heaven is my brother and sister and mother.'"

I love this. This is how Jesus felt about the level of leadership under Him. That's the priority Jesus put on people.

I tell folks all the time, "If you want to be close to me, go teach in the nursery." It's guaranteed that I'm going to come by and poke my head in that nursery and talk to all the workers. I talk to all the volunteers in the preschool classes too. I talk to every worker I can possibly talk to. It's kind of like a game. If I can talk to everybody, I win. And so I try to put in the time with my staff and my coordinators.

My sixth priority is ministry goals: corporate, individual, and personal. The church comes before anything I do on the outside. My next priority is immediate things to do. Both of those are considered highest-priority items. All other things are high and medium-level priorities. The more long range and further out it is, the lower the level of priority it is to me. Hobbies are near the bottom.

Lastly, I make time for my friends. I have a couple of friends—two brothers from Arkansas that married two sisters from Alabama that are just a lot of fun to be with. The two brothers were raised in the same house, but they're as different as night and day. One of them is a natural entrepreneur and is always talking about ways he can make things better. The other one also has great ideas, but when we ask him, "Why don't you start a business?" he always says,

"Why would anybody not want to work for somebody?"

When I'm with these two, I just laugh and have fun. They're really relaxing. Sometimes the three of us join up with our other friends—a conservative dentist and an old band cat who now owns his own seating company—and we go to a guitar show every year. The whole time we're together, we just laugh and laugh. It's hilarious what old hippies, a preacher, some rednecks, and a dentist can cut up about.

These are my priorities. Now take some time to write down your priorities. After your relationship with Christ and your family, which things are the most important to you? Once you have your priorities on paper, take time to pray and compare your priorities with the Word of God. Don't be afraid to ask God if those are His priorities, too, and if there are adjustments you need to make. It's only after I take care of my priorities that I take time to goof off (a lot of times your priorities can be mixed with fun and time with friends, so you're enjoying life all of the time).

Once you establish your priorities, find somebody that will hold you accountable. Maybe it's your pastor, a supervisor, a mentor, a friend, a coworker, or maybe it's your spouse; but find someone that will hold you accountable. For me, I have a group that holds me accountable, and they also depend on me for accountability. Many of the times the decisions that I make are because I know my family, my staff, my volunteer team, and the members of my leadership club are counting on me to not flip out. Not only them, all of my Timothy's (those who have answered the call to the ministry through my ministry) and the kids that I've taught over the years are also counting on Brother Jim to love God with all his heart, to love his wife, to love his kids, to work hard to serve his pastor, and to do the things that God has called me to do.

4. Develop a Desire to Change

Once you have your priorities set, it's time to stir up a desire within to change. The Bible says that God will give you the desires of your heart, so it all starts with your desire. You must get your *want to* right. And if you want the things of God bad enough and you have a desire to change, you will change.

5. Get the Right Tools

The fifth key to being organized is learning to master the tools you need to get the job done properly. We all know that we can pound a nail in with a shoe, but a hammer works better, right? And you can unscrew something with acrylic nails, but a screwdriver is really the better choice–not just any screwdriver, the right kind of screwdriver (a Phillips screwdriver isn't going to work everywhere). Having the right tools makes all the difference.

Everyone's list of tools may differ, but there are some essential tools that I believe no leader should be without. First of all, I believe with all my heart that everybody needs a calendar. Calendars are like lawn mowers—whatever size yard God has made you a master over, you need the right size mower (calendar) to be able to handle it. There was a day when I could handle everything I had going with a decade-at-a-glance. There just wasn't much going on. Every once in awhile I would just circle a date and write out what I had to do on that date.

Then I went to college and things started changing. And soon even a month-at-a-glance couldn't handle everything I was doing. I progressed to a week-at-a-glance, and then a day-at-a-glance. Eventually I had to break my calendar up in to minutes. From there I realized that writing in my day timer every moment was a waste of time.

My calendar has now evolved to an iPhone™ so I can not only record my schedule, but also check my e-mails. I can sync my computer with my organizer, and I don't even have to keep up with it. When that happened, my life changed. All of the sudden I was listening to a cacophony of alarms, buttons, beeps, and messages going off saying, "Whoops! You've got a meeting." I even set a reminder that says, "Go home." I'll be honest with you, when I'm working, I'll forget. But when that reminder comes up, I pack my stuff and head home.

Listen, your brain is not for remembering. That's your calendar's job. Your brain is for thinking and for dreaming— what a radical concept! Your calendar is for remembering, and if you fill up your head with all this stuff you need to remember, you'll never have time to think and dream like you need to. I don't remember anything—even when my wife asks me what time I need to get up the next morning, I answer,

"I don't know. Let me look at my calendar."

I want to master something that'll help me. Some would say, "Well, I'm not going to build a house, so why buy power tools?" But have you ever found that power tools, even on a small job, make a difference? The same can happen when you get a calendar.

Other people will argue, "Oh, I'll never use that thing."

Well, I didn't think I'd ever use an electric drill, but I do—and I'm not handy at all.

The next important tool to own is a watch. It's hard to manage time if you don't know what time it is. It's hard to show up on time, to end on time, or to do anything on time without knowing what time it is. I'm at the point that I wouldn't even know what day it is if it wasn't for my watch. Not only that, my watch tells me my hydration levels, my current elevation, and all sorts of other stuff.

The next important tool is a timer. I may be funny, but I believe that if you have a time to start, you ought to have a time to end. Every meeting I lead, I come up with an end time, and I stop when it's time to stop. When people call and say, "Jim, I need five minutes of your time," they talk pretty quickly because they know I've got a timer going.

One day I was at a store, and I went to use their phone. Over the phone was a sign that said, "Business phone. Please, limit calls to 3 minutes." And I thought,

You know, the phone on my desk is a business phone. Why don't I start limiting my calls to 3 to 5 minutes? This became my policy, and now if I talk to you over three minutes, I really like you. If I have a phone appointment, I allow fifteen minutes, but then I end it. I don't even talk to my wife very long—and I like her a whole lot! You can waste a lot of time if you're not setting an end time, and a timer will help you stick to it.

My wife even uses a timer when she's riding her bike. One timer tells her to eat, and another one tells her to drink. She's really little, and when she's cycling a bunch of miles, she has to eat and drink at certain intervals so she can keep her energy up. So when one timer goes off, I'll ask, "Time to drink?"

And she'll correct me, "No, time to eat," while she pulls out an energy bar and takes a few bites. Timers are essential for everyone.

Next on the list is a computer. I can't imagine managing a ministry without a computer, especially without Internet access. There are so many great ministry tools online. Plus, having your own web page opens opportunities to create pages that specifically help your group. In the near future, we're going to design a worker web page where all of our workers can log on and use the page like a resource library. If they forget a lesson or if they need teaching ideas or props, they will be able access a list of what is available to use at the church. Twenty-four hours a day, seven days a week, they can reserve props that they will need, or they can read through articles that help them develop their teaching styles. We will also post our newsletter and ministry blog that will cover ideas that other teachers have used. It will also be a place where my workers can post ideas they have.

Some may argue, "But there are dirty pictures on the Internet!"

Well, that's what they tell me, but I don't look at them.

Others may say, "Well, people talk to weirdos in chat rooms." I don't because I've never been in a chat room. I choose to post on forums out in the open before God and everybody. Also, I don't talk to women on the Internet, even the ones that e-mail me. I tell most of them to make a phone appointment, or I'll refer them to somebody else. The reason the Internet doesn't cause trouble for my ministry is because there are policies that I have established that I stick to. So, don't throw the baby out with the bath water. Get a computer.

Here's a radical concept. Get a cell phone.

I have learned that having a cell phone allows me to do more than one thing at a time. When I'm driving home, I return all of my calls for the day. That way, when I get home, I can just be with my family.

Being organized means having the right tools. When you have the right tools, you are equipped to handle more than one thing at a time, and multitasking will bring you to promotion.

6. Develop a Routine

The final step toward being organized is to develop a routine. At some point, the word *habit* developed a bad connotation. When someone mentions having a habit, we tend to associate it with something bad that needs to be broken. But not all habits are bad; some habits are good; in fact, some are really good. For example, washing your hands after you go to the restroom. That's a good habit. Closing the door behind you, that's a good habit. Putting on your clothes before you leave the house, that's a good habit. (That's also the law!)

As you organize your life, your family, your job, your ministry, etc., seek to begin developing the right kind of habits. One way I have applied this to my life is that I assign days and times each week to recurring events. There are meetings that I have with specific leaders that occur each week. Similarly, I'll plan times to look at the children's ministry classrooms and services to evaluate how they're doing. Other times I'll check in on the youth and college ministry services. Sometimes I schedule time to just see how our church is doing overall. When I schedule recurring events, it naturally develops a routine for me to follow to make sure I'm properly managing all of the departments under me.

I mentioned before that for years, I traveled a good bit. In one year, I'd travel anywhere between 100,000 and 150,000 air miles for conferences and seminars. On weeks that I didn't travel and just worked at the church, I started noticing (and this is crazy) that even though I had more days to work, I didn't have any meetings. That meant I actually got less done than when I was traveling.

Now, figure that out. I had more time in the office, but I was accomplishing less. So one day I asked my assistant, "What's the deal?"

She answered simply, "When you're traveling, you have a set time or routine for everything. You fly in and do everything in the same order to get it all done before you fly out again, but when you're home, you don't have a routine."

From that point, I developed a stay-at-home routine and an out-of-town routine. I found that once I developed that stay-at-home routine, on the weeks that I was home, I began accomplishing more than when I was out of town. I learned to just flip-flop back and forth. At one point in my career, I was in charge of the church's school, the children's department, and my team taught weekly at the church's summer camp. Even though the summer meant there was less to do for the school, I still had to go to camp once or twice a week. Even then, I had to establish a routine. So routines are not just for when I'm out of town or in town, they are for all of the different seasons my job takes me through.

One of the routines I have found works best in ministry (and leadership in general) is to take time immediately after we finish a big event to plan for the next one. If my event ends on Sunday, I'll take Monday and Tuesday off, but when I arrive for staff meeting on Wednesday, the first order of business is to plan the next big event.

The time to plan is when the event is fresh in your head. So, if you're doing a Halloween alternative, don't wait until the following August to start planning the next one. Get on it within a week of when it ends.

When the time for the next event draws closer, I'll pull out the file we made at the end of the previous one, so already I have different things established and done. I'm guaranteed to not make the same mistakes twice, and I remember all of the ideas my team had for how to make the event better. All of this is possible because of routine.

Keep Control

It's imperative that you maintain control over your schedule. Don't let your schedule control you. Treat your time like it belongs to you. If somebody says, "Hey, got a minute?" If you don't, don't lie. The same applies to phone appointments—learn to say no. Your time is valuable.

One way to control your schedule is to be selective about what you fill your time with. I used to have all kinds of people that wanted me to preach at their church or ministry, but if I said *yes* to all of them, my schedule would've worn me out. So I decided to come up with a form that each ministry had to fill out. The form told me a little bit about the ministry, and I coupled that with setting a ridiculously high price to sift out the non-serious people. The price alone did a lot of work for me—automatically separating the people that really wanted me to come and speak from those that just said, "Oh, let's just have any old guest in."

Another key to controlling your schedule is simply knowing what's expected of you. If you're going to be a multitasker, you must become a student of your job. Know your job description. If you don't have one, write one and run it by your boss. Don't be afraid to ask, "Is this what's expected of me?" Even if you're working in the ministry, write your job description and run it by the pastor. You'll quickly sift out the unnecessary tasks that are draining your time and your energy.

A job description defines what you are in charge of, and definitions are huge. In fact, this is where a lot of people in ministry mess up. Your idea of a good children's ministry and your pastor's idea could be two different things. Some of you work for a pastor who never talks about children's ministry; so you have to guess,

"Is this your vision?"

"Is this your vision?"

"Is this your vision?"

I know exactly what my pastor wants, and I know what he considers good ministry because I have a clear set of definitions he operates by.

When you have definitions, it levels the field of expectations and helps you avoid disappointment. For example, a lot of people will ask me what I think about various churches I've been to. The problem is that question is too vague; so before I try and answer, I always have them define what they think is a good ministry. If I say the church is really great, but they don't like that kind of church, they could visit and expect to really like the church, but they will inevitably be disappointed. So, once I know their definition of a good ministry, then I can answer in a way that they will know what to expect from that church and won't be disappointed when they visit.

When you make clear definitions for those who work under you, then you and your team's expectations will line up automatically. My problem is that I tend to expect more out of myself than even my boss expects. So I end up going overboard more than under-board. Some people have the other problem. Either way, it's important to make your definitions clear so that you can expect the same of your team members that they are expecting to deliver for you.

Finally, in order to maintain control over your schedule, it's important to understand the corporate philosophy: it's not just about you. You are working on a team. First and foremost, know your pastor's or your boss's heart. Second, study long-term employees and seek their counsel. They may suggest something beneficial that you hadn't thought of before. Next, listen to the voice of wisdom. Also, list everything that you need to manage according to your priorities. When you line your priorities with those above you, it will help you do more than you ever thought possible. And finally, evaluate constantly. Ask yourself questions such as:

1. What are my pastor's/supervisor's expectations and priorities?
2. Do I measure up?
3. Do I have the same expectations of myself that they have for me?

5

STEPS FOR GROWTH

If you have ever baked, you understand how important it is to make sure all of the ingredients listed on the recipe are included. Say you put all the ingredients in, but you leave out the baking powder. You'll still have a cake that tastes good, but it's going to be really flat. Time management is similar. There are four easy steps to managing your time, and some of you may already be doing some of these steps, but it's important to make sure you're not leaving any single step out. It could change everything.

Step One: Plan Ahead_____

The first step to being a time manager is to plan ahead. Everything that you plan for needs to go down on a calendar or organizer. But planning is more than just looking at the next twelve months and writing down what's going to happen on which days; planning must also incorporate your priorities. Before I plan the next year as far as what my ministries in the church will be doing, I plan how I can keep my relationship with the Lord growing and developing.

Then I plan the next year for my family. For example, when my girls graduated from high school, I knew I was going to be in the middle of the peak of my traveling schedule. Missing my girls' graduations was not an option, neither was missing a ballet recital, piano recital, etc. So, I always scheduled my traveling around the big things my girls were doing. Other family events I consider when planning are holidays, birthdays, anniversaries, etc. Like I said before, I have standing dates with my daughters. I also have dates with my wife. I still call and ask my wife out. I figure whatever won her affection is what will keep her affection.

Next, look at what meetings need to happen. And let me emphasize *need* to happen. I believe one of the biggest time wasters in the work world is meetings—we have meetings to see what meetings we need to have! So, I try to limit the meetings I schedule. In some of my meetings, we don't even sit down. We have standing meetings because then they'll end quicker. If I plan a ten-minute meeting, we'll just stand in my office, go through the thing, pray, and go. Sometimes I'll have a standing meeting scheduled, and I'll call off the meeting. Why? We have nothing to meet about. The problem was already solved or taken care of some other way. Remember that meetings are not limited to face-to-face encounters. Many times you can do the meeting by e-mail or fax.

Once you've determined the meetings you *need* to have, do them at the same time every month. Why? Because that helps the calendar challenged or the planning impaired. They can remember recurring items like "every third Tuesday" or "the first Friday of the month." I used to do this with my master teacher luncheons. There was never a question of when our meetings would be, and all of the master teachers could plan accordingly.

The other thing that I do when planning is something that I learned from my cute little wife Julie—appointments. I make appointments for everything that is important. Now, my wife is the queen of hair appointments. Because she travels with me and Yancy both, she's got it down to a system. She'll look at her itineraries and schedule her hair appointments based on the color her hair needs to be at one event or another. She is the queen of hair appointments. She didn't even own a calendar until a few years ago except to put hair appointments in it. The people that cut her hair stay several weeks booked out, so she has to have this appointment thing down to a science. As I was looking at her hair appointment calendar, I learned that I needed to start setting appointments for things that were important to me according to my priorities.

Some of you skeptics may say, "Oh, Brother Jim, you're not going to tell us you set an appointment with Jesus every day, right?" Yes, I do. But it's not necessarily at the same time every day. My life is not such where I can keep a 7:00 A.M. with Jesus. At the point of my ministry when I was in charge of both the school and the children's ministries, I had to lead a 7:00 A.M. meeting with the schoolteachers. Since the teachers had to be in class by 8:00 A.M., my appointment with Jesus was set for a different time. It's not that I put the teachers over Jesus; I just can't have a 7:00 A.M. with Jesus every day. Time with God is still my priority as long as I plan time with Him every day.

How do you keep your time with God a priority? For me, I have a reminder that comes up every night that says, "Before you go to bed, look at the next day, and set an appointment to be with Jesus." Some days it's before work, and other days it's during work. Sometimes I have lunch with Jesus; other days I may just read my Bible and pray while I'm on the treadmill— I'll be walking and praying that my heart won't jump out of my chest while I'm praying and studying God's Word.

Because the level of leadership directly under me is a higher priority than the rest of my workers, I spend more time with my staff, coordinators, and master teachers than I do with the little lady at the nursery window. Where I plan to spend my time is always based on my priorities, which makes decisions when writing a plan a lot easier to make. Which people, to-do lists, and events do you need to make an appointment for so you'll do what is important to you?

Remember, if you don't have a list of priorities in your life, you'll never keep them!

As you begin to put a plan and schedule together, look for a program or system that works best for you. Now, because I'm a computer guy, I color-code all my events. I'm a Mac™ guy, so I use iCal™. I have different calendars for everything, but I don't have to view all the calendars at once. With iCal™, I can click on whichever calendars I want to see, and I can follow what I need to because of the color coding. At a quick glance, I can tell if my day is full of children's, middle school, youth, or college ministry work. If I find myself really busy, I'll unclick things and see what is really causing me to be the most busy. Because of the colors, I can immediately pinpoint which activities I'm allotting the most time to.

Some of you may be thinking, *Brother Jim, I already do all that.* Well, then you are a good planner. But that doesn't make you a time manager.

Step Two: Think in Steps

The next step that will move you closer to being a time manager is learning how to prepare by thinking in steps. Now, this is what saved my bacon in college and kept me from flunking out. If I just wrote down all the due dates of the various projects and papers I had to finish, I wouldn't have finished college. I had to learn how to prepare for those upcoming due dates.

Remember the term paper due? Back up six weeks. I wrote in my calendar, "Go to the library and check out a book." The next day, I put another reminder, "Did you go to the library?" Two days later I wrote, "Start reading book." Now, this'll date how old I am. Since this was B.C. (Before Computers), next I'd write on my calendar, "Find someone to type my term paper." Since everybody's papers were due at the same time, I had to find somebody who was available to type my paper before it was due. Then I'd schedule, "Start writing term paper," and later, "Find someone who speaks

English to proof term paper." It was all about preparing, step by step.

I follow a similar routine to prepare for my wife's birthday. It's not enough to write "Julie's birthday." I have to back up a week, and write, "Go to store. Buy card." And that's not it. I'm a man. Men will buy the stupid cards, but then they'll forget to sign them. And so I have to write, "Sign card. Make dinner reservations. Order flowers. Buy present." And as the date approaches, I write, "Remind girls it's mom's birthday. Give girls money for mom's birthday."

The same thing is true if you have vacation Bible school to plan. It's not enough to just write down when vacation Bible school starts and finishes. Back up nine months and write, "Pick a curriculum or a theme"; later, "Appoint coordinators"; and finally, "Announce dates." You must always think in steps.

A lot of people ask, "How'd you find time to write articles for all the blogs, plus work on other publications, and write your own books while running Jim Wideman Ministries, working at church, and spending time with your family and friends?" It's simple really. I put a due date on everything I want to write, and then I schedule various appointments to write. When it's my appointment for the day, even if I don't feel like writing, I still do it. Sometimes I don't feel like going to the doctor, but I still make appointments to see him.

A few years ago I wrote a chapter for a book for Group Publishing about twenty-first century children's ministry and the trends that I see developing. I didn't just jump in and start writing it immediately. I figured out when writing the book would be a priority, and I set a due date and appointments to write. When my other priorities were taken care of and the appointments to write came up, I would just sit and write. And when the timer will go off and say, "Quit writing," I'd go do something else. I finish all my writing and ministry assignments that way.

This is one thing that a lot of calendar people don't do. They'll write down when their newsletter is due, but they don't back up and say, "Write newsletter." But those reminders are key.

Another form of thinking in steps is to write to-do lists. Assign a category to every to-do list, set the priority, and assign a due date. Once I've scheduled something I need to do, I set it up to repeat until the due date or until Jesus comes back, whichever comes first. For example, my church's all staff meetings are on Tuesdays at 9:00 A.M. And so, I have my calendar set to remind me every Tuesday about staff meeting. When it asks me when the appointment ends, I click *repeat*, always! What if the only time someone can meet with me is on Tuesday at 9:00 A.M.? I say *no* because my calendar says, "All-staff meeting" every Tuesday at 9:00 A.M.

Additionally, not only can you set appointments to repeat, but you can also change the priority level. And you ought to. There are some things that I think are high priorities, but after a couple of days pass and I still haven't done them, I see they really weren't that high of a priority. Sometimes, I'll change the priority to a lower level, but sometimes I just go ahead and press *delete*! Since it was supposed to be done a couple of days ago and I've lived without doing it, I figure I don't need to do it at all. A good time manager constantly looks for items where the priority level can be changed, can be deleted, or can be delegated to someone else to do. We'll go into more detail about that a little later.

Do you set the priority level on your to-do list tasks? Do you adjust the priority level if necessary? If your answer is, "Well, sometimes I do," ask yourself if that makes you a time manager. I'll tell you the answer. No, that just makes you a good calendar keeper.

Step Three: Evaluate_____

The third step is what separates time managers from the expert calendar keepers. Evaluation. Remember when we talked about maintaining our checkbook registers? Your finances would be really messed up if you never wrote down how you spent your money. Well, when you evaluate your time managing skills, you have to actually write out how you spent your time. Note, I did not say to write down how you *wanted* to spend your time, nor how you *planned* to. How did you *actually* spend your time? At the end of each day, take time to compare how you actually spent your time compared to how you wanted to. When you take time to do this, you can easily identify timewasters.

I realize that there are times you are called to meetings that you didn't plan for, but there's nothing you can do about that. When those things happen, take some of the things you were going to do that day and assign them to someone else. Or use your time to do something else. The more you evaluate, the easier it is to identify how to spend your time, even when the schedule changes.

Timewasters may seem small and insignificant in the midst of your daily schedule, but think about this: If you can save 1 hour a day for a year, you've given yourself 15 days (more than 2 weeks) of 24-hour days. Now, if you break those 15 days up in to 8-hour workdays, that's 45 eight-hour workdays (6 weeks and three days) of time in the office you've saved with just one hour a day. If you save 2 hours a day for a year, you've given yourself a month of 24-hour days or (in office time) the summer off—3 months of 8-hour days. That's pretty good.

I'm constantly looking at ways that I can change my schedule to eliminate time wasters. And usually they're not even big earthshaking things. For example, I quit watching the six o'clock news when my kids were little. Rather than come in every day and tell my girls, "Don't talk to me. Daddy's watching TV," I decided I wanted to spend time with my kids. If the country bombs someone, somebody will tell me. I went through the whole O.J.-trial without watching anything, yet I can tell you everything that happened. People will always tell you stuff, so why would I sit there watching TV, when I could be playing dolls with my youngest daughter? And because I had time to play dolls with her when she was little, now she makes time for her dear old dad to sit down and tell him what's going on in her life. It's the neatest thing in the whole wide world.

Recently, Yancy, my eldest, was preparing to teach some workshops. I've pretty much always done her little computer presentations. At the time, I was really busy with the school and church stuff I was in charge of, but I still called her and said, "Hey, you got your notes done?"

She said, "Yeah, I've got my notes done."

So I told her, "E-mail them to me, and I'll do your presentations."

I could hear the surprise in her voice when she said, "I wasn't going to ask you because I knew how busy you were, but since you asked, I'll let you do them." An unskilled time manager wouldn't have had time to do the presentations. But because I had worked to eliminate time wasters, I still had time to do the little things that were a priority to me.

Now, I admit after evaluating my schedule, I have found some meetings that I probably didn't need to have. There are some other things that I change and some that I can't. But that doesn't diminish the value of evaluating how I've spent my time.

Once you've identified time wasters, you can start looking for ways to improve yourself. Take time to figure out how you need to spend the time that you're saving. Maybe it's doing something for your family. Maybe it's starting a new ministry. Maybe it's bringing in some extra income. I don't know, but the Lord will show you. The key is to not stop after you've planned and prepared, go ahead and move on to evaluation. It makes all the difference in your time.

Step Four: Delegate_____

The final step to becoming an excellent time manager is to master the art of delegation. Delegation is simply appointing someone to represent you. When you delegate, you have access to the time of others which opens your time up for more important tasks. What are you doing that someone else can do? Use the time of others, and always look for opportunities to build a team.

Some may argue, "But, Brother Jim, I'm so important that the things that I am doing I just can't entrust to others."

Listen, I realized years ago that I'm not the only person that can straighten the chairs. I'm not the only person that can check the wireless mic and see if it has a battery. I'm not the only person that can do certain tasks that I thought I was the only one who could. The person who says,

"Well they can't do it like me," has forgotten that there was a day they couldn't do it like someone else before them. Somebody let you sorry all over a group of people and get better. And somewhere, you're going to have to make a list, give it to that sound man, and let him come in and do all those things. Guess what? He will do it just like you as long as he follows your list.

The people you delegate to will excel if you understand one principle, people don't do what you expect, they do what you inspect. Delegation needs definition along with it. Any time you delegate without defining how you want it done, the task will develop a weird spirit. It won't have your heart. When you delegate to someone, have them turn in a checklist detailing what they did, and leave room for them to write comments to you. As soon as they write a comment like, "Need wireless batteries," you have an opportunity to write back and say,

"I'll get them. Thanks so much for what you do!" When your delegate reads this, they'll understand that you really do inspect what they do. And as you continue to help organize others, the Bible says, you'll receive a righteous man's reward. What are righteous men's rewards in your church? Their time and their tithe. You bless them, train them, and take good care of them, and they will help you do the work of the ministry.

What are you doing that someone else can do? I've already told you a couple of things. Maybe you need to quit setting up your room—write up a set-up sheet for someone else to follow. At my previous church, there was a written manual for nursery workers, another one for preschool, another for elementary, and one that covered our pre-youth ministry. Those manuals answered the questions workers ask such as, "What do you want me to do?" and "How do you want me to do it?" These manuals were filled with job description of positions we knew someone else could do, so we wrote the policies, got the forms, and made it all accessible to our workers.

Let me ask you a question, if you had a thousand head of cattle, would you feed them all yourself, or would you get some other people to help you with the feeding process?

Delegation naturally leads to building a team. So as you begin to delegate, ask yourself these questions:

1. What are you doing that's keeping you from doing what only you can do? Identify those tasks or duties.
2. If delegation is someone representing you, where do you need to be represented?
3. What are you doing to put in to others so you can use their extra time?

Now, being a kid of the 70s, I learned a valuable lesson from Three Dog Night,

One is the loneliest number that you'll ever do
Two can be as bad as one;
It's the loneliest number since the number one.

I want you to understand something. It's true in love, and it's true in ministry: you're never going to get everything done until you build a team. You're never going to have fruit that lasts until you build a team. Ministry or business is not rocket science . . . Love people. Teach them to use what they have to offer, and build a team!

I study the Trumpster—Donald Trump. In fact, when I watch *Apprentice,* I consider it one of my continuing education classes. The Trumpster says, "You cannot be successful if you don't build a team." This was clearly illustrated in one of the previous seasons of the *Apprentice*. The finale came down to two women. The woman that won hasn't been seen since. Really, the other one was a better candidate, but she didn't win because she didn't build a team. She was down on her team all of the time, and when it came down to making the final decision, the panel sided with the one who understood teamwork. Even though the woman who lost was more qualified, her lack of teamwork cost her the show.

Think Big

Now, if you'll manage your time effectively when you're business or ministry is small, you'll be forced to do so when you're business or ministry is big. And if you manage your time well, your business or ministry will get big. Let me tell you a real quick story.

In 1990, I was working for a church in Oklahoma, and when I wanted to use a bus for an upcoming event, I just hollered out my office door, "Anybody using the bus Friday night?" If no one answered back, I assumed (and I emphasize the word *assume*) that I could use one of our two buses. The bus never had gas in it. It was never clean. And most of the time, more than one person thought they had reserved the same bus for the same night.

I knew that wasn't a good way to operate things, so I sat down and said, "Alright, if we had a fleet of buses, how would we have to operate it?" My team came up with a form and policies; for example, when you use it, you clean it and fill it up, etc.

Over fifteen years later, the ministry operated over a hundred vehicles and employed full-time mechanics to maintain them. You know what's funny to me? When I left that church some seventeen years after I started, we were still using the same form that I made when we had two buses. All because I sat down and said, "If I had a fleet, how would I run it?"

But, Brother Jim, I don't have a fleet!

If you start managing things well when you are small, you will get big. That's some of the best advice that I could pass on to you. Whether it's a business, ministry, or volunteer team, learn to manage your time well, and watch as it grows and grows.

One area that I treat as bigger than reality is my volunteer teams. I treat my volunteer interviews the same way a CEO of a major corporation would. How do I know? When I watch *Apprentice,* I pay special attention to my favorite part—the final four. At that point in the game, CEOs of major corporations interview the finalists. I rip off more interview questions from those episodes than any other time. I call that selective creative (but I'm highly selective about what ideas I borrow).

Double-Sized Techniques_____

Stop looking at your business or ministry the way it is; see it the size you want it to be. To me, double is good, so I want to always ask the question, "What would I need to do if I was leading double the team I am now?"

There are many simple ways to begin treating your business or ministry like it is double its size. Here are a few policies I have found most effective:

1. Have people turn in weekly reports. Some may argue, "But they're volunteers!" Yes, but they're also coordinators that are responsible for doing something. Inspect what they are doing by checking out what was actually done.
2. Help your workers prioritize their projects.
3. Limit meetings. Whenever possible, communicate in writing. When you do schedule a meeting, have an agenda. State the purpose of the meeting, and don't let people get away from your agenda.
4. Spend time with people, individually and corporately.
5. Make people take time off. I've found when I'm at my busiest, I need to take a few days and go find a hot tub and get in it. Your workers should do the same. (Remember, even convicts get time off for good behavior!)

6. Make things easier for your helpers.
7. Offer help.
8. Streamline and simplify.
9. Be willing to change. We're creatures of habit. We like doing it the way we've always done it. I have to constantly tell my volunteers that we're rethinking things to save time. And when they start to grumble, I remind them that I'm not married to anything but Julie. We have to kick some stuff in the head and change it. We're always going to have to do some stuff differently.
10. Find equipment and technology to help you do things quicker or more effectively. It may cost more money on the front end, but it'll save you money later.
11. Learn how to do more than one thing at a time—multitask.
12. Study what others do that works. Be a student of what others do that actually brings success.

6

BUILDING YOUR TEAM

As I've mentioned before, God never meant for you to do the job alone. Doing it all yourself doesn't bring fruit that remains, so every great leader must be an excellent team builder. My favorite story to illustrate this is found in Exodus 18—the life of Moses. Beginning in verse one, we see that Moses had a measure of success, but because he did the job alone, there were problems at home. In the previous chapters, we see that there were so many problems at home that Moses' wife finally just told Moses that she was going home to daddy. So she did. She took the kids and left.

We don't hear that story cited often. Instead, we hear about Moses parting the Red Sea and leading the children of Israel out of captivity. But because he chose to do those jobs alone, it caused tension in his family.

When I became a father-in-law for the first time, I did a study of great father-in-laws of the Bible. One man who stood out was Jethro. Jethro's name means "excellence," so if Mr. Excellence came to see you, would you listen to what he said? That's the dilemma that Moses had. A man named Excellence came to see him, and he happened to be his father-in-law too.

Jethro did some very wise things. The first thing the father-in-law did was send his daughter—and the kids—back. Wise father-in-law. In verses fourteen through eighteen, Mr. Excellence doesn't just take his daughter's word for it—another trait of a good father-in-law. Jethro went and watched. He listened to what Moses had to say, but then he also went and looked at it. Afterward, he told Moses, "Listen, what you're doing is not good for you, and it's not good for the people." That shows that Jethro was a man of wisdom. Any other father would've said that it was not good for his daughter, too, but he didn't say that.

So what did Jethro tell Moses to do? Take more time off? Learn to play golf? No, he said, "You handle the hard things, but then, train the people. Teach them. Allow them to help you. Some will be captain of ten, fifty, five hundred, some a thousand. They'll help you in different ways." Mr. Excellence told Moses that the key was not to just get better at doing his job; he needed to build a team.

The Bible tells us that Jesus had the Spirit without measure when He left the wilderness. And we know Jesus had a pretty fair healing anointing in His ministry, didn't He? Jesus was full of the Holy Spirit. He was the original Body of Christ. He had it all, every part. But yet, the first thing He did when He started his earthly ministry—He recruited help. Listen to me; if Jesus needed help, we need truckloads of it.

Duplication Versus Delegation_____

Delegation is the act of empowering to act for another, or representing someone; a group of persons chosen to represent others. We need people to represent us, We really do.

But delegation is not dumping. Somewhere we've gotten it into our heads that as soon as we find someone to represent us, we just throw him or her into the job and lock the door. Three years later when we've recruited another delegate, we open the door to throw them in, and the previous delegate runs out yelling, "I quit," And then it repeats over and over. You need people to represent you, but delegation without duplication will not bring fruit that lasts.

Duplication is the act or process of duplicating, the quality or state of being duplicated. What does that mean? A duplicate is an exact copy of an original. How many of you would rather have people help you, or people just like you to help? See the difference?

Through my years in children's and youth ministry, I have had certain leaders who have filled other classes with their helpers. Why? Because while I wish I could just lay that worker on a copier and make copies, I have to stick new recruits in their classroom. Then after that leader inputs into the recruits, teaches them, and shows them the proper way to lead a class, then I come back in and say, "I'm back to get my recruits." And I take them and give them their own class.

What happens to the original leader's team? They get some more greenhorns, and he or she trains them up. I put my heart into that level of leadership. They put their hearts into the next and the next and the next. The difference is that duplication is where the blessing comes.

One thing I know from SEC football is that there is a difference between having a position covered and having depth at every position. The people with the most depth are in the championship. You can have a good first string, and you can have a good second string, and that's a great start. Having two strings is impressive, and I'm sure I can learn something from coming to see your classes work. But what separates the good ministries from the great is that there are second, third, and fourth strings. And when you're forty-eight points ahead, you let that true freshman get up and teach the memory verse. Then you're developing.

During the early days of my ministry, when I finally recruited an assistant praise and worship leader, I would only let that person lead when the worship leader was gone. But they never got really good. Why? Because the praise and worship leader was gone only about three or four times a year, and that's the only time the assistant leader led. I realized the assistant wasn't going to grow by just filling in for only a handful of times a year, so when I came to Tulsa, I established a policy that assistant leaders would lead once a month; and if it was a five-Sunday month, they'd do it on the fifth Sunday, too. It was amazing how my second string got better.

Then, once my second string was well developed, on that fifth-Sunday month, I started developing my third string. When you combined all of my leaders from the various classrooms, I really had twelve or fifteen strings going at the same time.

After a number of years, I had a farm club system established for the kids. Most everybody in our adult main service praise and worship teams came right out of our own fifth and sixth grade classrooms. They played their way right up to the main service. You see, the farm club can work in more than just major league baseball.

My teams weren't restricted to just praise and worship. I started applying that to all branches of ministry as well. One of the coolest things for me to see was when one of my former ushers, who was twelve when he was in my classroom, was promoted to head usher over the adult service at my church. In one church I worked at, I was there long enough that I went to staff meeting with kids I once had in children's church. They remained in the church helping, blessing, and doing a tremendous job. None of this could have happened without duplication while I developed my team.

10 Steps to Duplicating Yourself in Others____

1. **Identify every position where a worker is needed.** How are you going to duplicate somebody if you haven't identified the position that you have for them to serve in? This is what I don't understand. If you're going to identify a position, identify every single spot. But you say, "Brother Jim, we're just so small right now. We don't need all of those positions."

Listen, if you don't even have the one position filled yet, what are four more under that position going to hurt? If you're still looking for the one, and you've got to believe God, you might as well believe God for the whole thing! So the key is to identify every single position. As you're identifying your positions, consider this: If finding workers was not a problem, where would you use them?

2. **Create job descriptions.** In each job description, identify the gifts and abilities needed so you can be specific about the type of people you need to fill each position. Now, you may ask why you can't just do the job description once the person gets there? Because God will give you what you make room for. One of the secrets of church growth, and one of the things that has always worked for me, is to make sure you're always ready to handle growth. We see an example of this when Jesus did His first miracle at the wedding in Cana in Galilee. What would've happened if those guys had only filled up the water pots halfway? That's how much they would\have received. The fact that they filled them to the brim opened the door for them to receive all that they needed.

   Also, whenever someone made room for God in the Bible, there was always some physical work on the part of the person wanting to see a miracle take place. Jesus could have turned air into wine just as easily as water. I mean, the whole earth was created by the spoken Word, so He could've said, "Let there be wine," and that would have been that. But He wanted to prove another point—if you'll do what you can do, God will do what you can't do. He'll work on your behalf.

   Finally, as you are making room for miraculous growth, the Bible explains that there is always a step of faith on the part of the person receiving the miracle. In the wedding in Cana in Galilee, the step of faith the people had to take before they saw the miracle manifest was to bring the cup they filled with water over to the master of the banquet.

The Bible doesn't say when the water turned to wine, but I know when the Lord works in my life, He's never late. He's seldom early. And I have a sneaking idea, and this is just me, but I think the water turned to wine when the servant let go of the cup. Once there was a step of obedience and faith, then snap! God stepped in and did what the servant couldn't do.

Another example from the Bible is found with the story of Jesus feeding the 5,000. I don't care if you use a little boy's lunch or a catering truck, there's got to be organization and planning involved in feeding that many people. And think about it, what's the first thing Jesus did? He took inventory of what they had to work with, the little boy's lunch. The next thing He did was tell the disciples to arrange the crowd into groups of fifty. Why? You can tell if fifty people have eaten or not, but you can't tell if 5,000 or more have eaten. He had a physical plan. Nothing miraculous. Nothing outstanding or supernatural. He just got the people in groups of fifty. Fifty over here, fifty over there. After He carried out His plan, He blessed it.

And finally, the time came for the disciples to take a step of faith. They had to take the bread to the people. Just the twelve of them were going to use the boy's lunch to feed everyone. And when they did it, the food multiplied as they were handing it out. I don't believe that all of the sudden they were standing in front of a warehouse full of food. First they had to act in faith, and then God blessed them. God's also the God of leftovers. He had enough for another day for folks to be blessed.

Once God begins to provide the people to fill your job descriptions, remember to keep people in the right place. Sometimes people confuse unity and union, but there's a difference. God not only made body parts to have different gifts and functions; He also placed certain body parts where they would never have fellowship, yet as long as they're on the same body, they're in perfection union.

For example, if my forehead ever sees the middle of my back, surgery is about to take place. But you know what? As long as those two things do what God created them to do, they're in perfect unity; but if they ever form a union, it is not pleasant. For example, my nose and my armpit do not need to form a union. There's a reason why your nose is not right there by your armpit. In the duplication process, the placing of parts is just as important as filling the various needs your ministry or business has.

3. **Have a way to discover interests, gifts, and abilities.** One of my favorite tools is a volunteer worker application. If you have to have an application to flip burgers at McDonalds™, you ought to be able to have an application to get to know people. Some say, "Brother Jim, we're in a small-town church. We already know everyone." Well, you may think you know everyone, but it's not just the crazies from big cities making the nightly news. Even small towns have crazy stories about messed up things that are going on after dark. Just because it's little, it ais't necessarily good.

Use the worker application to also see how much experience the person has. Be careful, and don't take their word for it. Just because they write, "I did such-and-such at Brother So-and-So's church," doesn't mean it's true. I always call Brother So-and-So and find out if the applicant was a blessing or a curse at their church. I'll be honest with you. There are some people that have gone to my church and worked under me, and when they decided to go their own way, I helped them pack.

When they got to their next church, they said, "Oh yeah, we were over at this other church and worked with Jim Wideman." Most churches don't call to confirm that they were workers, or good workers at that. They just assume the person is telling the truth. But, if they would have called me, I would have saved them some heartache. As you're building your team, take time to check folks out, and do reference checks. A worker form is for more than just weeding out the crazies; it's a way to discover interests too. The primary purpose of the form is to find out what somebody likes to do. If they just write something generic like, "I want to help wherever you need me," I either give that application to somebody else or have someone call them back and find out exactly what they want to do. I need to know what they're interested in because if I don't put somebody where they have interests, they will not stick around.

Find out their gifts and abilities. How do you do that? Start them small and move them around until you find their niche. See which gifts rise to the top. In my book, *Volunteers That Stick*, I go in to a lot of detail about why so many workers I've led have stayed in service for a long time. The primary principle for making volunteers stick is to find that person's gifts and interests, no matter how many different areas they try before they're successful.

Some leaders are worried about hurting the worker's feelings by letting them try something, fail, then moving them to try something else. But, setting someone up to fail will also hurt their feelings. Setting them up to win might be a little embarrassing when you move them, but in the long run you'll be doing them a favor.

4. **Create an organizational structure.** Now, one of the things that I believe with all my heart that is so important is to put your structure on paper. One of my favorite The Far Side™ comics is the one with a bunch of chickens lying outside their coop. The

grass is covered with these motionless chickens that almost look like blobs, and the caption below says, "Boneless Chicken Ranch." That reminds me of a lot of organizations that don't provide a skeletal system. You can have little chicken lips, little chicken heads, chicken legs, and all kinds of other little chicken parts, but if you don't have a skeleton to put it all together, it can't move anywhere. The same is true with your business or ministry. The organization you establish is very important.

Write your structure down on paper. If people were no problem, go back. You've identified the positions. You've looked at their gifts. You've looked at middle-managing and coordinator positions. Where do you need people to represent you in, not only responsibilities, but also in the area of authority? There is no responsibility without delegated authority, so you have to delegate authority along with the responsibilities.

Your skeleton should define which parts are connected to which, and it should also clearly lineate who's in charge of each responsibility. When you give someone a little responsibility, give them some authority too. For example, my nursery director doesn't have to tell a parent, "I'm sorry, but since your child has a fever, we can't bring them in the classroom." Instead, I have given that authority to the check-in lady who can stop them up front and doesn't need to wait for the nursery director to answer each call. Things like that need to be put down on paper.

Another key to developing a sound structure is to be willing to move your people around. Through my years of ministry, I've had to deal with being understaffed a lot. When that happens, I start asking, "Alright, who do I have that's really strong that I can move over here?" Then I put some people with them, and many times I don't have to recruit anybody. I just have to move some workers around to fill the need. Other times I've had a teacher just go nuts and recruit like crazy: all those who were kin to her, everybody that works with her, and everybody she knew were all recruited to help in her class.

When that happens, the tendency is to say, "Well, don't break up that team." But I say *yes*! Break up that team! And tell them to do the same thing that leader was doing. Go get everybody you're kin to, everybody you know, and just multiply.

Remember, put it all on paper, and make sure that your organizational structure is a growth structure.

What's the difference between a growth structure and a maintenance structure? One causes you to go to another level. The other allows you to stay stuck.

It's similar to weight gain: once you buy the bigger pants, you grow into them. That's why in my own lifetime, I have purposed to only buy a certain size of pants. That's as big as I buy. I either have to lose weight or go naked when I get to that size. And it's against the law to go naked, so that's it. I know what'll happen—if I buy the next size, *pfff*! My current pants will be too tight. It's the same thing with structure.

Some children's pastors have prayed, "Lord, give me a hundred kids in my ministry." Then they structure their services to accommodate a hundred kids, but when they get to about 75 or 80, they just hover there. They may have a big day and over a hundred kids show up, but soon after that, the numbers go back down. Why? It's a statistic that in America, 75 to 80 percent is full. For example, in America, a seven-passenger minivan generally only holds five Americans. That same minivan taken into Mexico averages 12 to 15 people in it. Take that minivan to Uganda, where I was a few years ago, and they install racks coming down the back and on top. On one minivan in Uganda I counted thirty-one people in it and on it—a seven-passenger minivan.

Churches in America are getting stuck because they don't change their structure. You can change the seating arrangement, but your church won't fill up. You've got to change your structure.

I've also found over the years that you don't need the gift of discernment to figure out structure; you need a calculator. In the churches I've worked for, percentages pretty much stayed the same no matter how large or small the church was. For example, the number of preschoolers to adults always hovered at the same percentage. The same was true with any demographic such as the number of nursery or elementary kids.

I have also watched the ratio of workers in different places. As the church I'm working for grows, when the pastor starts talking about what size the church is going to grow to, I can run the numbers and see how many of that will be preschool, elementary, etc. I can also look at the present ratio of students to teachers and use that to figure out how many more teachers I'm going to have to recruit. You'd be surprised how few people ever just get out the calculator and run the numbers of what they need to recruit and what they need to duplicate and what they need to handle.

5. **Put your heart into your workers.** Why should God give you more workers if you're abusing the ones you already have? If you're not taking care of the ones you have and you're not spending time with those workers putting vision into them, then why should He honor your attitude toward them? One of the first sermons Jesus preached was about attitude. It's important that you start putting the right heart into workers, because if they don't have the right heart when they're recruited, they will develop bad attitudes and bad habits.

How do you start putting your heart into workers? Spend time with them. In order to disciple someone, there is always both a disciple and the one who disciples. Communicate your vision visually in newsletters, brochures, and everywhere else that you can. Let your workers know both your vision and the plan you have to make it come to pass.

People follow people with a plan. Here's what I know about Americans: you give them a hero and a cause, and they'll rally around that person. Every good general has a battle plan. Every successful entrepreneur has a business plan. Every good football coach has a game plan. And somewhere, you must have a plan and start putting that plan to action; teaching folks to work your plan, making corrections and adjustments, and looking for every opportunity you can to put into people.

If you don't get anything else from this book, remember this: the time you put into other people is never wasted. It is the best time you or I could spend. It's more important than what you're reading; it's more important than the conferences you're attending; it's more important than anything else.

One of the practical ways I put into people is by taking an interest in what people tell me. For example, if somebody tells me that their grandmamma is sick, I note that on my schedule, and I make a reminder to ask that person about their grandmamma the next week. I'll also put in a reminder to pray for her. So that next week, I can ask that person how their grandmamma is doing and let them know that I've been praying for her. And I'll tell you what, that means more to my people than anything else. Love your people, and they'll love you back. It's so important.

6. **Start spending time with the level of leadership directly under you.** Now, I can't spend the same time with everyone, but I need to put time into the level of leadership under me on a regular basis. My key staff, coordinators, master teachers, etc. are the ones who

get the most time with me. Even if they're volunteers, it's important that you treat them like you would your employees, and give them some of your time.

The first way to spend time with your leaders is in regular meetings and communications. I do a lot of luncheons where I just teach and put my heart into people. The hard thing about a multiple-service church is not getting workers; it's getting all the different services with different personalities to move in the same direction. Because of that challenge, I try to have a representative from every service in those meetings, so we are all moving in the same direction. That is really the key to developing longevity.

Another way to spend time with your people is to do something thing I believe a lot in—have fun! When I was in Tulsa, my church would have a lot of fellowships—meetings just for the workers and their families to hang out and enjoy each other. I always had a great turnout for these kinds of things. And during that time, I would walk around and spend time with folks and talk to them.

I also make it a habit to always take somebody with me wherever I go. I don't like to drive, so I often try to bring somebody to drive me. They think they're just driving me, but I'm putting into them. I teach them what I know, or I explain why I did something a certain way. I really enjoy those times when I can input into my key leaders.

A different way to give your leaders your time is to encourage them to ask questions. I love questions. I do. I tell my staff that when they aren't asking questions, I'm worried. I want my leaders asking me questions. One of my previous interns was puzzled when I told him this, so he asked me,

"What questions should I be asking you?"

That was a good question. I explained that I wasn't going to give him which questions he needed to ask me because if the question didn't really come from the person, that person's never going to learn.

One of my professors in college told me that a growing faith is a questioning faith. There's a difference in a question and a doubt. But I know when I start asking, "Well, why do we do it that way?" or "What's the real benefit?" or "Is there another way to do this?" those kinds of questions will always cause me to go to the next level. Anytime the people under me aren't asking those kinds of questions, I say, "Guys, we need to be thinking of some more questions right now." Otherwise I can't tell what they're learning.

Jesus is our prime example, and He not only allowed questions; He asked some Himself: "Who do men say that I the Son of man am?" (Matt. 16:13 KJV). I have used Jesus' example to ask similar questions about my ministry through the years. For example, I'll get on a leading children's ministry's resource website and look around for what people have said about conferences I taught in, or if they're talking about coming back the next year. Sometimes I can find people's opinions on the positive aspects of the conference, and sometimes the negatives. All of this information helps me answer the question, how can we improve and grow? When your leaders begin to ask those questions, you know that you are successfully duplicating yourself in them.

7. **Model how you want the job done.** One of the methods I have used that has made my teachers better teachers is that I don't just throw them on stage and tell them to teach. I don't just coach them and say, "Okay, next time you can improve in this, and you can improve on that." It all starts with a model. Every part of our service is being modeled by someone who knows how it is supposed to be done. My new teachers always have to take time to see how ministry is performed, and it makes all the difference.

And it's not just the person preaching the sermon that needs to model; it's all areas of ministry. For example, one of the hardest things for a volunteer to do is to emcee a service, keep it flowing, and not have any dead spots. Emceeing can be learned, but it's got to be modeled first. And once my new worker has seen a number of good models, then I let them try it. I don't just hope for the best. I make sure my leaders are watching, constructively critiquing, coaching, helping, and encouraging along the way. My paid staff is responsible for critiquing and coaching and encouraging as well. We all attend one service in our multiple-service weekend, and we spend one service walking around and inspecting. This is the Santa Claus management that I was talking about: make a list, and check it twice.

Every week when I walk the halls of the church, I can usually find about 12 to 36 things that need improvement. I believe that if you can walk in a room and only see a room, then you do not have the gifts of a Head Fred. A Head Fred can walk in a room and see more than just four walls: he sees opportunities, and he sees room for improvement.

The reason modeling works is because *showing* is better than *telling*. My models are modeling more than just how to teach, They model everything. I, myself, model everything as well. Sometimes I take a staff member with me and model how to walk and inspect. And while I'm explaining to them what I'm looking at and pointing out things that need to be improved, they'll comment that they hadn't even noticed these things before. Everything needs to be modeled.

Ministry is like a checkbook. If you don't make deposits, you can't write checks, So, we've got to make spiritual deposits: we need to go to church, have quiet times, read the Bible, and do other things that build up your spiritual account. But at the same time, if you're just attending services and hoping everything works out; your account is going to run out. You must model, and you must evaluate.

8. **Make assignments and let others work under direct supervision.** This is where coaching comes in. Make a checklist, Observe, And be sure to become your teachers' and helpers' biggest fan. This is key. As you are training and coaching your leaders, catch people doing things right and brag on them. If every time you talked to someone you only told him or her something negative or something he or she could improve, that relationship would not be very strong. Strong leaders point out the good things, make corrections, and move on.

9. **Make corrections and adjustments so that it's done your way.** When you make corrections, make corrections gently. Don't just say, "Just do it this way!" Explain why you want it done that way. When you do this, you're duplicating yourself because you're letting them see your heart.

   One of the greatest things I believe that you can do is to allow your leaders to solve their own problems. This is how I do it with my key staff: I tell them, "Don't come to me with problems. Come to me with three solutions to your question, and I'll tell you which one of those solutions I want you to do."

   After they've done this for awhile, I'll start saying, "Alright, which one of these three should I pick?"

   But they already know the answer, so they'll say, "Oh, I know you, Brother Jim. This one right here."

   What just happened there? I just taught them how to solve their own problems. And now they solve them just like me.

10. **Promote workers and increase responsibilities.** Once you do all these things, you have successfully duplicated yourself, and now it's time to increase responsibilities.

"But my people don't want to be increased!" Sure they do. Everybody wants to do a better job. And once they find out that there is a place to be promoted, they're going to work harder because people want to be promoted. What I have volunteers do at my church is the same thing that a lot of full-time people are paid to do.

At one point in my ministry, I had another children's minister ask me how I did everything I was doing. I only had eight paid staff members, and he had thirty-six; but he had about 500 less children in his children's ministry than I did. I explained to him my philosophy: my staff's job is to manager volunteers, not to be paid teachers of classes. If you want to have less staff, boost your volunteer base.

As you promote people and increase responsibilities, then all of the sudden you allow them to start putting what they know into someone else. And that's where the duplication process multiplies. Now your heart is being transferred into other people.

The Fruit of Duplication

When I walk through my church's halls, I'm always blown away when I see people that I have never met in classrooms doing things just like I would. I put my heart into somebody else, and my same heart was taken by them and put into somebody else and then somebody else. In fact, it doesn't even start with me. Everyone in the classroom is a reflection of my pastor and his vision for the children's ministry. When you duplicate yourself, everyone in your ministry or business naturally moves in the same direction and does the same thing.

Duplication isn't just your responsibility. Everyone should be a part of the duplicating process. You should be a duplication of somebody else, and you should also be duplicating other people. Ideally, everybody under you should be putting into someone as well for the duplication process to be complete.

One of the biggest benefits to duplication is that you never run out of workers because there is always a fresh bunch coming up. This may sound rough, but one of the best things that happens around here is when a worker moves away or quits. I know that usually goes against logic; but when it happens, all of the sudden, my assistant teachers will take over, and folks will move up, and positions will shift. But with that shift is an excitement and a momentum; and all of the sudden that new leader is ready to take what they've been learning and go at it. The outcome is always positive.

You know that it hurts people's feelings when they quit, and you say, "Good." But if you've properly duplicated yourself in that area, you know the transition is going to be just as smooth as it can be. That is the key. When the duplication process works like this, then you're always going to have enough workers.

Start Duplicating

Now that you've got an idea of how this copy machine works, you may be wondering where to start. Remember, it all starts with having a plan. Ask yourself these questions, and write down the answers to get the duplication process started in your life.

1. **What areas are you presently over where you need to be duplicating?** Another way to look at this is to ask yourself where you need to be delegating. Where do you need somebody to represent you? Where do you need another you?

2. The next question, and this is where a lot of people blow it, **what workers do you have now that you see potential in?** I didn't say, "Who do you have that can do it?" Who do you just see potential in to be better leaders? Stop only looking for the "just add followers"

people. I know, we all want instant. We live in an instant world: instant grits, instant macaroni and cheese, everything's instant. And we're looking for all this instant stuff, but yet, it's okay to find somebody that just has potential. Who do you see with potential that you can invest in? Time you invest in someone else is never wasted.

3. **What are the key positions where I need depth?** I don't know why it took years to come up with the assistant-master-teacher concept. My church had the master teacher process, and things were working, but eventually we came up with a process to cultivate and make more master teachers. I needed that at the same time we had the master teachers, but it took us several years before we implemented it. The problem was we didn't have anybody trained that could put depth into the assistants, and until those master teachers were in place and doing what they needed to, then I couldn't have people that could put the depth in key positions. You don't need depth everywhere. There are never that many kids going to the bathroom, so I don't need my bathroom people duplicated. But there are some other areas where you do need some more depth, and you need to identify those areas.

4. The last questions is, **how can I free up and manage my time so that I can start the duplication process in other people?** As a leader, the only way that you're going to have and build the team that you want to have is if you can free yourself from things you're doing that someone else can do so you can spend time with your leaders.

Building Your Dream Team_____

If you're building a sports team or a church team, which positions are needed? What are the skills, gifts, and abilities needed? Choose your team wisely and match the gifting with the position, and again, spend time with your team on a regular basis.

When I was working in Oklahoma, I found that even though I was the Christian Education director, I was spending more time with adults that I was with the kids. Ed Young, Jr. says, "The bigger the ministry, the more time you'll spend in leadership." And it's so true. So when I was wishing I had more time with the kids, I would ask myself,

"Do the kids love me?"

Yes, I had a relationship with the kids, but I still had to spend more time with the adults. It's important that you realize the bigger the ministry, the bigger the business, the bigger anything in your life; you've got to spend more time in developing people and not just doing the work.

Now, if this is true, why do we end up spending most of our time on daily or routine tasks? Maybe that's why we don't have the team that we want to build. So, with that in mind, I want to give you some steps that I use to multitask, so you can do more than one thing at a time and do them all well.

7

STEPS TO MULTITASKING

The first step to multitasking is to develop a routine that includes time to develop others and to accomplish what you should do. Every week I have meetings set with key workers that I duplicate and put in to. Sometimes these meetings are in my office, and sometimes we go out to lunch together. But all of these meetings are scheduled around a weekly routine I have with my key staff. You, too, must develop a routine; and part of what you do every week should include developing and putting into other people. That's something only you can do.

Secondly, you need to take time to master the tools that give you the ability to multitask. I was so happy when I upgraded to an iPhone™. With just my phone, I can now read my Bible, check my calendar, write e-mail, pull up office documents, and do presentations. I no longer have to rely on free wi-fi in the city; so I can do anything online from any place. This is a great tool for allowing me to do more than one thing at a time.

Also, I don't know why anybody has a desktop computer. I'll be real honest with you. I couldn't function with a desktop. Having my laptop, knowing that I can set it up anywhere, do work anywhere, do presentations, etc. is worth the extra money, even if I had to pay for it out of my own pocket (which I had to do when I got my first laptop).

Next, you need to start depending on to-do lists and reminders, otherwise you will forget things. Even if you try to remember them, you'll forget. But if you have them written down and reminders set, you'll never forget anything again. With to-do lists and reminders, all you have to do is to check your to-dos and accomplish them according to their priority levels. It makes all the difference in the world. Also, you need to daily update and change the priority of each task, so you're not doing things that aren't as important as the other things you should be doing.

Another step to multitasking is to always look for ways to evaluate and improve. Those are two things you can do anywhere. For example, if I am in children's ministry, I can constantly say, "Alright, how can I learn from this? What can we change? What can we improve? How can we do things better?"

I mentioned before that I like making people ride with me in the car so I can control the conversation. On the way to lunch, I'm setting up the discussion; while we're eating, we get into the heart of the matter; and on the way home, we're finishing up the discussion and figuring out the things we need to do. You've got to drive to lunch anyway, might as well work.

I also make sure people don't take the conversation off-topic. If they start talking about their favorite football team or something, I shut that down really quickly with something like, "We don't talk about nobody but the Crimson Tide in this car," and then we just go on and talk about what I want to talk about. I figure whoever buys gets to control the conversation. So, if I'm buying, you better be quiet and talk about what I want to talk about, okay?

Additionally, if you are going to be a multitasker, you must read, study, and grow. One of the things that I try to do is make time for personal investment, so I always keep a book with me. I make goals at the beginning of the year concerning how many books I want to read, and most of the time I'm able to keep those goals. I once heard Leon Fontaine speak, and he said that he read a book a day. Wow, Leon became my hero that day; I'm not that good. But I can do a book a month. For awhile I used to read multiple books at the same time, but in order to meet my goal, I had to quit that. So instead of reading different books in different places, I usually buy two copies of the same book and put it in different places. Then I keep up with which page I'm on by noting it on my phone.

Not only will I read a lot, I'll buy books for other people and tell them to read. Then we'll talk about the books. One of the things that I do on my weekly report is ask my key staff what they're doing for leadership development (going to church doesn't count). This way I'm making sure that my staff is constantly reading and growing too.

But these kinds of things will help me to learn to multitask because every time that I can read, I try and find something else I can do at the same time. A lot of times I get caught up on my reading in the off-season for cycling because I'm on stationary bikes. Don't worry; I don't read on my real bike. I just ride on it. But I'm always looking for ways I can do more than one thing at a time.

Here's another thing that really helps me. Network with others. Find out what's working with other people. There are several people that I call on a regular basis and just ask, "What's going on? What have you seen? What's working? What's impressed you? What have you read about? Tell me what you know."

I have some young guns throughout the country that will let me know when they're going to conferences, and they will act as my eyes and ears at different places. I know that if I show up, people won't tell me what's really going on. They won't talk to me about what doesn't work. To be honest, I don't understand that. I'll tell you what didn't work. You ought to tell me what didn't work. But I've got some of my Timothy's (those in ministry that grew up in my ministry) that will go to these things, and they'll network and be my eyes and ears.

Sometimes, I ask our guest speakers to come in a day early just so we can network and talk about what's going and ways we can tweak some things. Then I'll hook them up with some of my small group people so they can pick the speaker's brain about how to do certain things. Yes, we bring folks in to teach at conferences and special meetings and events, but at the same time, if we can learn about how to disciple new converts or how to get people into small groups better or hassles with multiple-location services, then I'm multitasking by taking advantage of the time that speaker has at our church. You have to learn to network on a regular basis. Blogs are another great way to network. Go to www.jimwideman.com and click on my blog. You can also see whose blogs I am reading and learning from a little farther down my blog roll.

Moreover, as a multitasker, you must encourage the ideas and opinions of others. As a leader, it's really tempting to go ahead and answer every question, but I have found that if I'm going to train others, I need to encourage others to share their ideas and opinions. There are times when you have meetings just to go over business that you've got to go over. But you should also have time in meetings for others to share their ideas. Some of the best ideas that I've ever had are not ideas that I had. They're somebody else's ideas, and after they told them to me, I ripped them off. So, there you have it.

Finally, evaluate your structure as well as your actions. This is one of the things that I started doing and has really made a difference with my team. While I go through and evaluate my day and evaluate what's done, I also evaluate the organizational structure at the same time. In other words, I continually ask, "Is this a growth structure or a maintenance structure?" And while I look at how I'm spending my time, I'm also identifying places where I need to enlarge the structure or places I've ignored that need attention. And when I evaluate, I'm looking at other projects at the same time. So even in your evaluation, evaluate multiple things.

CHAPTER

8

DOUBLING YOUR LIFE

What would happen if your ministry or responsibilities doubled? Would you need more space? Would you need more workers? Would you have to order more chairs and desks? How many of you would have to have a little more help from an organizational standpoint?

Alright, here's a radical concept; <u>D</u>o each one of these things I just told you, and you'll double. Enlarge it before the people are there, and the people will show up. Delegate to those you've duplicated yourself in. I know, letting go is the hardest thing in the world. But you've got to do it.

When I was in Montgomery, Alabama, I loved to lead praise and worship. I'm an old guitar player, so I'd play my guitar and my daughter would jam along with me. I've always loved jamming with my family. Well, in this church, I had duplicated myself in every other area of the children's ministry except praise and worship because I took care of that myself. I had my puppet directors, Sunday school teachers, Wednesday night workers, <u>E</u>verything. After I left the church and moved to Oklahoma, I remember calling my old church and asking, "How are things going?"

"Well, do you want us to be honest?" they asked.

"Well, yes, I want you to be honest," I replied.

"Everything's going good, but we have a sorry praise and worship team thanks to you." From that moment on, I purposed in my heart that I was going to not just do the things I enjoyed doing, but I was going to duplicate myself in those areas as well.

In my next church, I still played in the praise and worship band but only on Wednesday nights in the fifth and sixth grade classroom. It was a little band that I filled with handpicked buddies to play with me. That was my gift to myself, and boy do I miss those folks and those times! I have been faithful in the small things, and God has made me a ruler over several Taylors™, Gibsons™, and Fenders™; so I played like I was playing Fillmore East. But I also started another band in training, so when my band wasn't there, there was still a decent praise and worship team to lead. Once you duplicate yourself in all areas, then you've got to step back and let people do what you've trained them to do. That way you are freed up to only do the things that God wants you to be doing.

It's a domino effect. When you allow the leaders under you to take responsibilities that free you up for more important things, soon the leaders under them will begin to do the same. Once that process begins, you'll find yourself with more time than you've ever had to do what only you have been called to do.

Top Ten List for Time Managers_____

If I could only do ten things to make the best use of my time and to be the manager that God has called me to be, here's what I would do:

1. **Account for your time.** Get in to the habit of writing down how you spent your day and evaluating how you spent your time. Ask yourself: Was this the best way to spend my day? Was this the best use of my time?

Is there something else I could be doing? Is there something I'm doing that somebody else needs to do? Are there a bunch of small meetings that I could combine in to just one meeting?

Now, once you've spent your time, it's gone; but you can make changes so that tomorrow is better. Write down how you spent your time, and evaluate it.

2. **Plan *your* time offensively.** Notice that *your* is in italics because it really is *your* time. It really changed my life when I realized that my time belongs to me, and then I started acting like it. I started by making some policies for how I spend my time. For example, I don't do business in hallways. At my age, when I'm going to the restroom, I'm going. I'm not going to just stand there and talk. Sometimes people don't know that's my policy, so they'll call out, "Brother Jim, Brother Jim!" as I walk by.

"Sorry, see my executive assistant (Betsey doesn't like being called *secretary*). Get an appointment. Send me an e-mail." I just keep walking. It may sound mean, but I'm spending my time according to my priorities. This is especially true when I'm on my way to meet with my pastor—my pastor is a higher priority, so I don't allow others to take my time away from him. You've got to be willing to start planning your time like it belongs to you. Learn to say *no* to the right things.

3. **Keep your priorities in order.** If you don't have priorities, you can't keep them. The key is to number all the items on your to-do list according to your priorities. Once you have them numbered, make sure that what you're doing has the highest priority.

4. **Delegate to the faithful.** I hope that through all this talk about duplication and delegation, you are committing to let go of some of the things that somebody else can do. That is the best way to free you up to do the right things. Got it?

5. **Plan for interruptions.** I learned this years ago. When everything is said and done, there's a lot more said than done. Things don't actually happen the way you plan for them to happen. There has been many a day when I've called my wife, and she asked, "How did your day go?"

"I don't know, baby. I haven't started it yet."

"Well, it's time to come home," she'd encourage me, and I'd respond,

"Yeah, it's time to come home."

Now, when I was younger, I would stay and crank it out a little bit. But I've found that when I'm tired, and if I'm a little frustrated or irritable because I didn't get to do what I planned on doing, then the best thing I can do is kiss it all goodbye. It'll all be waiting for me in the morning. I can either go love on my family, I can let them love on me, or I can go get on my bicycle and pedal the stress away.

Another key when preparing your schedule is to not plan your day and only leave five minutes to yourself. Basically, you don't want to get so booked up that you don't allow for interruptions. If you have a day that's just one appointment after another, people are bound to get irritated when you get off schedule. That's why I only do phone appointments one or two days a week, and the max I can do in one day is three. That's it. I can't handle taking calls every fifteen minutes just to answer questions about random things.

I also like to keep a little variety in my schedule. If I know I'm going to be tied up in the morning doing interviews or something that has me sitting down, then I'm going to schedule myself to do something active in the afternoon like running errands. But the most important thing is to remember that interruptions will happen, so leave your schedule open enough to plan for them.

6. **Respond, rather than react, to a crisis.** Another great thing my mother told me is that there is more than one side to every story (and I've found that in church work, there are about thirty-seven). Because of the truth of this statement, you just can't act on things as soon as you hear them. To respond involves getting some advice; whereas, to react means just letting your emotions decide what to do about the problem. The thing with reacting is that most of the time you're making decisions when you don't even know the whole story. There's nothing wrong with saying, "I'll get back to you. Let me look into this." I've learned that if you'll just do some homework—talk to some people—then you're not going to have to say *I'm sorry* nearly as much. That's something that I think is very important.

I also learned from one of my professors in college that the smartest answer you could ever give anyone is "I don't know."

Say it with me, "I don't know. Let me look into it. I don't know."

When I was in Oklahoma, my church hosted large children's ministry conferences. Since I was the director, my face was the first one you saw in the brochure. And because of that, I had people coming up to me all the time and asking me questions I didn't know the answers to. So, I'd say to them, "You know, I don't know, but let me ask."

They didn't know it, but the person that knew more of the answers was someone whose face wasn't even on the brochure—my assistant. So we would go and find her, and she knew the answer right off.

Now, if I said, "I don't know, and I'm not going to help you find it out. Just figure it out yourself," that would be wrong. When you answer, "I don't know," be sure to also offer to help point that person in the right direction. Sometimes you have to say, "I don't know anybody that knows that, but I'll find somebody, and I'll call you this week and let you know." Now is the time to get in the habit of doing that.

7. **Don't procrastinate.** Do what you can do, and don't put it off. Learn how to do more than one thing at a time. I use my speakerphone whenever I can so my hands are free to work. One of the things I loved working with was this nice little gadget that served as a wireless earpiece for my desk phone. It was the coolest little thing. I would hit this little button, and it would lift up my receiver so I could talk. Plus, I could walk around the office and do things while I was on the phone. The only bad thing was my secretary thought I was talking to her all the time, so she'd answer me. But then she'd see the thing in my ear and realize I was on the phone.

Another tip is to always take advantage of wait time. People will always ask, "Can I put you on hold?"

"No!" But it's too late; you're already there. Use that hold time to get something else done.

If I'm in a waiting room, instead of reading some crazy magazine, I've got my phone or my laptop so I can go over documents, check my e-mail, evaluate, return messages, check my voicemail, etc. Anytime there's downtime, I'm looking for those kinds of things to do. With this in mind, always have something to do or read with you.

A good goal concerning procrastination is to set a standard response time to return all calls and e-mails by. I want to be known as one of the best responders to e-mail in the world, so I have practical personal goals. For example, I want anybody that sends me an e-mail to not have to wait more than eight hours for a response. And, it's really cool when I can do it in a lot less than that. Within twenty-four hours, I try to return all calls. If I can't return the call personally, or if I'm still looking and I don't know, I'll have someone call and say, "He still doesn't know, but he hasn't forgotten about you." That goes a long way.

Now, I'll be honest with you, I don't like to type. That's a bad thing for a guy that does hundreds of e-mails daily. So, if people ask me multiple questions or long questions, then I send them an e-mail back saying, "Please make a phone appointment." I can talk a lot faster than I can type, and at least they've received a response from me. The key is to not put things off.

8. **Get some help.** One of the things that I do on a regular basis is find out how other people have done what I'm about to do. You don't have to reinvent the wheel every time there's some sort of big decision or project for your team. Find out how another group has handled the same situation. Call and ask a different leader. Listen, usually the leader's assistant knows that stuff, so just call and ask. You can also read a book or subscribe to a podcast. Get a mentor. Join somebody's club. I lead a children's ministry leadership club, and the primary purpose is for other children's ministers to learn from what I've done so their time can be focused on ministry and not how to handle situations. Again, don't try to reinvent the wheel, okay?

9. **Plan for growth.** Now, we talk all the time about planning, but what do you actually plan? For example, if you're a children's minister, what is your plan for kids' spiritual growth? Do you have one? Do you have a plan for organizational growth? It's not just a matter of figuring how many workers you need, but have you come up with a plan for how to get them? How to train them? How to duplicate them? Have a plan.

What about numerical growth? I guess I should've been a salesman, I don't know, but I just like having a goal. My youngest daughter sells cosmetics, and she loves being a makeup artist. It's something she's always wanted to do, so every day she comes home from work telling me how much she loves her job. It's so neat seeing her so happy doing what she wants to do. But the one thing that I love most about her job is that every day she has a sales goal. And every day, I ask, "Did you make your goal?" Usually she tells me how she went over her goal, or how she hit her goal before she went to lunch.

I've learned that if you don't have a plan to grow in an area, you won't grow in that area. So make a list of all of the areas your team needs to plan for growth, and sit down and develop that plan. People follow people with a plan. Maybe the reason why you're not getting the results you want is because you don't have a plan to achieve them. If you don't make plans that generate new growth or expansion, and you aren't ready to follow-up when you begin to grow, don't expect much to happen. It's time to come up with a plan for all of those different areas.

10. **Increase your prayer life.** The last thing that will help your team more than anything is to use some of this extra time that you now have set aside to increase your prayer life. I believe the Lord can do more through thirty seconds of prayer than we can do in a whole day of work. Allow Him to help you.

When you are sensitive to the leading of the Holy Spirit, it's easier to follow those little leadings. For example, one time I was leaving my house to come to work, and I just heard deep within me bigger than life, "Bring your bass."

I thought, *That is crazy. I've got to stop eating pizza late at night. I don't need to bring my bass.*

But I knew I had heard, "Bring your bass."

Now, it wouldn't have been earth shattering for me to bring my bass. Plus, if it turned out that I didn't need it, I wouldn't have listened to that voice again. But, I decided that I didn't need my bass, and I just came to church. As soon as

I walked in the office, the guy who plays on Wednesday night called and said,

"Hey, I just got to work and found out that I've got to work late. Can you play bass for me tonight?"

My helper, the Holy Sprit, wanted to save me from going home and coming back on a busy day. He already knew, but I didn't listen. You know, that is where we blow it most of the time. It is not the "Sell all you have and move to Africa" messages that we miss. We usually hit that one. Where we blow it sometimes is in that still small voice.

Whether it's big or small things, it's so important to follow the Holy Spirit's leadings in every choice you make. As I look back over my career as a children's pastor, most of the jobs that God led me to, I was not qualified for. In fact, recently I came across my resume that I used before I got my job in Tulsa. At the time I was not qualified to do the jobs I eventually did at that church. Boy, am I glad the Lord didn't let that stop Him. He knew I could take the job, grow with it, and He would open doors to bigger things than I could have imagined. For example, this past Easter, my church saw around 20,000 people come through its doors. I constantly have to lean on the Lord to help me because I don't know what to do when God moves bigger than me. But even though my resume may not reflect my ability to do those big things, I know that it's vital to hear the voice of God and do exactly what He says.

"Thus saith the Lord" works every time. I have never had to apologize for doing what the Word says. If you'll do what the Word says, even if you don't feel like it, and if you'll obey just because you know that's the right thing to do, it will pay off. It's like eating green beans. If you don't eat them, you won't get the nutrients. But if you swallow them, you'll get the same benefits as somebody that loves green beans when they eat them. The green beans don't care; you're not hurting their feelings. They're going to give you nourishment every time you swallow them. And just like that, the Word will work every time you use it.

It's Not About the Hours_____

I know some people complain, "I work 70 hours a week," or "I work 90 hours a week." But, listen; if you'd quit counting all those hours, you'd probably get a lot more done. It's not about how many hours you spend working each week; it's about what you accomplish that counts. Don't even worry about the hours. Just work. And when you're done, go play.

George Barna says that time is the new money, and I've seen this. When I started in youth ministry over thirty years ago, if somebody paid five dollars to go to an activity, you knew they were going to show up. But I have kids today that sign up for some activity, and they put down 15 to 20 dollars, and the families will just blow that off and don't show up. They don't even want a refund! Something will come up, and *pff.* They just don't show up. Time is more valuable to them than money. So that's why it's important to keep track of your time and accomplishments like you keep track of your money.

About five years ago, I started doing some one-on-one leadership-development coaching and personal-time-management evaluation. One of the most eye-opening exercises that I do with these people is to sit down one-on-one and analyze their schedule. They write down how they spend their week, and I go over better ways to use their time, or I tell them how I would spend it. Most people don't believe that anything they're doing qualifies as a time waster, so I point out things that they're doing that they can eliminate.

A lot of what I know about adjusting my schedule I learned from reading about other people's schedules. My favorite part of Donald Trump's books is where he details his schedule for a week. Rudy Giuliani also reveals his schedule in his book on leadership (I started doing standing meetings because of that book). Every time that I can get a hold of someone's schedule, I find ways to evaluate and tweak my schedule to be more efficient.

As I have studied other leaders' schedules, I've learned that one attribute of a leader is to think quickly on his feet.

People are always going to have troubles and unexpected events, but the leaders are the ones who know how to respond and know what they can do to help. Take a look at your own decisions concerning your schedule. Why do you choose to do those things? Is that the best use of your time? What are some ways other leaders have prioritized their schedules? The best choice you can make as a leader is to evaluate your schedule on a daily basis and look for ways to improve it.

9

SCHEDULE OF A MULTITASKER

Maybe some of you are reading this book to get an idea of what my schedule is like so you can learn from it. I know that over the years I have had a lot of people from my leadership club ask me, "What does your schedule look like?" The truth is, it's a constantly evolving life form, but back in November of 2004, when I was at one of the busiest seasons of my life while working in Tulsa, I thought it'd be fun to record how I spent a few days of my time. So here's a glance at my schedule from when I was working as a Christian Education director, school superintendent, and a department head over a couple of other ministries in my church.

Sunday: First thing, I got up and started getting ready for church. I had my quiet time in the process of getting ready and was out the door in plenty of time to stop at Starbucks™. Several years before that, I started buying supper for some of the Starbucks™ employees on Sunday nights, so I would stop by the store on my way to church to pick up some coffee and to see who was on the schedule to work that night. I started this to build relationships with people and as a project to win people outside of my church to Christ. I believe that everyone should be trying to win someone to the Lord, even if you work in a Christian environment and are surrounded by Christians every day. My plan was to adopt that Starbucks™ and get everybody saved. And it worked.

Once I left the café, on my way to church, I checked my voicemail. Now, that may not sound like much, but even though I'd only done two tasks, I'd already checked five things off my to-do list, and I had some coffee. I arrived at the church forty-five minutes before service and started making my rounds. Since I was over the parking lot and security, I started by checking to make sure the department was ready for the service. Then I went by pastor's hospitality, my office, checked my box, signed anything that needed to be signed, checked my e-mail, and then headed to the Resource Library (where all of our props, copies, and snacks were taken care of for each children's church class). I double-checked how it was running, and, at the time, we were reorganizing, so I also made sure we were progressing in the reorganization.

From there, I walked through all the children's classrooms, monitored how the check-in procedure was flowing, greeted teachers, and observed what was going on in our hallways. By this time, I'd already made a list of things I could work on that week. Next, I checked in with key staff to see how things were going. I visited with church people along the way and bragged on workers every chance that I got.

Since I was over hospitality, I checked on the coffee carts set up in the walkways, and then I made my way to our valet parking services. Then I checked in with security one more time, went back to pastor's hospitality, and I visited with my pastor to see if he needed anything from me. We ate breakfast, went over announcements that I was to make in the 9:00 A.M. service, and stayed as long as my pastor was talkative. When he started to get ready for service, I put on my microphone, went to the restroom one last time, and went to service.

During the service, one of our cameramen passed out. Since he was the husband of one of my nursery service coordinators, I made a to-do in my organizer to call and check on him through his wife later that week. (If he hadn't been related to one of my workers, I would've let our pastoral care department check on him.)

I did announcements in the service, visited with people afterward, and recruited some folks. Every week I'd set a goal of how many people that I would try to recruit to work in the children's department. I even carried little cards to give to people to fill out to let me know what they're interested in. Later in the week, I'd pull those cards out, figure out where they wanted to work, and mail them an application. You see, that was part of my plan. Remember, if you don't have a plan, you won't grow.

Next, I checked with security on the status of the cameraman who passed out. Now, I wasn't checking on the cameraman, I was checking on security to make sure we called the ambulance and took care of the man. At that point I was looking at it from a liability standpoint. I wasn't being a children's pastor at that moment; I was being the head of security. I was making sure all of my departments were taken care of.

From there I checked on my pastor's family in the speaker's room. At that time, since I was over the vehicles, too, I got my pastor's wife's car keys, so my vehicle department could take care of some problems that she was having with her car. I touched base with the vehicle people to make sure it happened. I checked on valet parking one more time to see how the lots were clearing for the next service, and then I went and observed the pick-up process in the children's ministry classrooms.

The 9:00 A.M. service was all about looking for ways to improve and achieve greater goals in all of my departments. So, the next service at 11:00 A.M. was all about observing the classrooms in the children's department, making a list of improvements needed, and noting what people were doing right. After that service, I went to my office, checked my box, signed whatever needed to be approved, and continued my day.

A lot of times, people become bumps in your streamlining process because the process of getting what they need approved takes too long. I've found that if you can make the approval process as quick as possible, then people are going to get what they need, and things are going to flow. It's important to constantly streamline the process and not let things sit for very long. One way I streamlined the flow was to make sure I checked my box and signed anything I needed to (check requests, P.O.'s, etc.) every time I came in or left my office.

At that point, I started checking with my staff on where they were on their assignments for that night's meeting to train workers for our upcoming Christmas event. Everybody that I didn't see live, I called on the phone. Since service was over, I was also walking through all the children's classrooms to see whom was left and what was going on. I thanked every worker I saw for their help that day, and I let security know that I was leaving the property so they could contact me on my cell phone. After one more ride through the parking lot just to see what was going on, I drove home.

On my way home, I called my wife to let her know I'd left the church. (That was our code to let her know she could start making lunch or put something on the grill). I checked my voicemail, and I called my girls to let them know I was headed home and to find out where they were. We always have the girls and my son-in-law over for Sunday lunch. In fact, my wife still cooks, and we still do that every Sunday. It's the highlight of my life, and it's really fun.

When I got home, I changed clothes because I'm a food spiller, and I started my time at home. When I eat lunch with family, they have every bit of my attention. After lunch my wife started watching a NASCAR race (she's a big fan), and my daughters started taking naps. When everyone was napping, that was my cue that it was safe for me to get on my computer. I pulled out the laptop, checked my e-mail, and began studying for that night's meeting to organize the Christmas event. I also worked on my calendar and spent time planning, preparing, and evaluating. When the family started waking up, I closed my laptop and spent time with them until it was time to go back to church.

I arrived at church an hour before my staff because I wanted to see what condition everything was left in. Then I started helping set up. This sounds kind of crazy, but I have found that if you can look for ways to take the load off of your staff, then they're going to look for ways to take the load off of you. I tell everybody that works for me, "I got some good news and some bad news, and they're the same thing. I'll never ask you to do anything that I'm not willing to do. That's the good news and the bad news because I'm willing to do just about anything."

While everything was being set up, I looked for anything that was forgotten. Now, this is where I'm a little bit of a micromanager. Rather than fuss at everybody because something's not done, I'd rather fix it myself. Then I'd add it to my checklist to tell the staff later that week, so it wasn't forgotten again. Some people just like to fuss about what was forgotten, but they won't fix it themselves. I like to fix it first and fuss later.

Once everything was set up, I had time to visit with volunteers as they arrived and thank them for helping. Then, the training began. After the meeting, I evaluated the event and started making notes for next year's training—ways we could improve. My staff met in my office just for a few minutes so we could discuss how the meeting went and what we could do better the next year. After we discussed what we could improve, I took time to brag on them, especially, on my brand new assistant. That was her first year to coordinate the 1,300 volunteer jobs that I had to organize for our Christmas event.

I dismissed my team, checked my voicemail and mailbox, and then I went on a date with Whitney, my youngest daughter. After dinner, I took Whitney to Starbucks™ for coffee and to deliver dinner for the employees. From there we went home and spent the rest of the evening with the family.

Before bedtime I once again checked my e-mail, looked at my calendar, read a little bit, talked to my wife, and went to sleep. And that's a non-busy day for me!

Monday: The next day, Monday, was my day off, but because of the Christmas stuff going on, I still had some things to do. I woke up, talked to my wife, read a little bit, and had breakfast with the family. Whitney and I went to Starbucks™ and the chiropractor. On the way, I checked in at the office to see what was going on and took some time to talk to Whitney. While waiting at the chiropractor, I read my Bible. On the way home, I talked with Whitney about her world and just tried to find out what was going on with her. Then we went to Barnes and Noble, and I bought five books. From there we went to the grocery store for my wife and got stuff for lunch. I checked my e-mail while my wife prepared lunch, and then we ate together. After lunch, I helped Julie and Whitney decorate our Christmas tree, and then I packed for my workout. Since this was right after my bike accident happened, I went to get a massage first.

I checked in the office after the massage, and then worked out. I had a personal trainer that I used two times a week, and it was a real blessing to me. He helped me with my health, and as a bonus, I was able to read a lot of leadership books while I was doing cardio. I also got an idea for an upcoming lesson for my leadership club during my cardio workout. I made sure to write down my idea after the workout, and from there I returned five missed calls on my way out. All of the calls were work-related and needed me to help solve problems. On my way home, I called my family to see if they wanted a smoothie, and along the way I ran into my son-in-law. So, I took him out for dinner and just loved on him a bit. It also gave me a chance to encourage him about the new business venture he was launching.

After dinner, I went home and spent some time with my family before everybody left. Yancy had a band gig, and Julie was running sound, so they all went to band practice.

Whitney went to ballet, and I left to go buy a battery for my heart-rate monitor. While I was out, I saw two of Whitney's friends and had a chance to visit with them and counsel them on new relationships. Then I saw two other people who used to go to our church, but I did not spend any time with them. Why? Because I spend time with the most productive people, people who are high on my priority list. Just because I know somebody doesn't mean that they automatically get some of my time.

Now, this is something I've learned. My church's key staff members don't do a lot of the church counseling; we do some but not the bulk. We let some of our other very capable staff members do biblical counseling, and other types of counseling we refer out. The key staff, who happen to lead teams of people, try to spend their time with the most valuable people in our church. Who's that? The helpers, the workers, the ones that are doing really well. Our main job is to help those who are doing well, do really well.

A lot of church counseling appointments center around the counselors giving them the Word, and then the counselees spending the rest of the appointment explaining why the Word will not work in their situations. Many times, the pastor has recently preached messages on their situations, but one of the reasons they have a problem is because they aren't coming to church very often. So, why should I spend my time with the least valuable people in my church when I have a worker that could go to a new level, get his own class, or take off in a situation and do something big if I just spent a little extra time with him. I'm looking for the most productive people to spend my time with.

After my trip to buy a battery, I came home and worked on this book. I checked my e-mail, went over re-enrollment forms and policies for our church's school, and read one of my new books until my family came home. When my family was home, I focused on them until bedtime, and then I read and prayed with my wife. Whitney had some friends over, so I spent a little time with them, and then I went to bed.

Tuesday: The next day I woke up, read, got ready, had some breakfast with my wife, and then went to Starbucks™. (I went to Starbucks™ a lot, didn't I?) Then I checked my voicemail on the way to work and called my mom. I try to call my mom on a regular basis; I'm a mama's boy.

When I arrived at work, I had an overview meeting with my key staff from all of the departments I was over. This meeting was conducted standing up—a standing meeting. We went over things that they needed from me, what needed to happen that week, things that I needed to know, and any updates for the week's schedule. Usually after that I would have an individual meeting with each staff member, but we cancelled that because of all the Christmas preparations we were dealing with. Instead, I worked on helping the departments get ready for the Christmas event. Any time that you can help somebody else, it's the best thing you can do.

I went over the Christmas event recruitment and plan of action to confirm the volunteers. Because of the enormity of this event, I frequently found myself preaching to my staff my philosophy that "we can do this no matter what else we have to do." As we continued to discuss all aspects of the event, I would dismiss staff members when I was through with them. I figured that if they didn't have anything for me, and I didn't have anything for them, why should I make them sit through a meeting that has nothing to do with them? The best thing I could do was release them to go work. What a radical concept!

After the meeting, my CE staff and I looked at immediate things that needed fixing from Sunday, and I made assignments pertaining to what needed to happen for the Wednesday service. Then I signed all check requests and P.O.'s, answered voicemails and calls, and checked e-mails. From there, I headed to our church's camp to prepare for the Christmas event.

On the way to camp, I went over the state of our elementary children's church classes with our children's pastor, assistant children's pastor, and the intern that was in the car with me. We talked about recent volunteer leadership changes and a recent staff change. We also discussed strengths and weaknesses of each class and what we needed to do to coach and lead each one. We made assignments and a plan of action. Now this is just on the ride to camp.

Then we went to lunch. I bought lunch so I could direct the conversation. I focused on each one of them individually and got caught up on what was going on with them. I even opened up and shared a little bit about myself. We laughed and cut up and had a great time. Once we were back in the car, we went over our game plan for what we wanted to accomplish while we were at camp and what each person was responsible for. When we arrived at camp, we split up and got after it.

Now, some people like to have their team work like the Department of Transportation—one guy with a shovel, three people watching. I'm not like that. I would rather give everybody a shovel, tell everybody to get after it, and get it done in just a quarter of the time. I'm silly that way, but if I can hurry up and get home, I can see my wife. So that's what we did.

Before we left camp, we made a list of things we still needed to do. Our lists covered everything from walkthroughs for the Christmas event to brainstorming with the team about what needed to be done Thursday and Friday while people wrapped up the week. Then I checked in with my secretaries (I had four at the time because of the number of departments I was heading up). And then we hit the road.

On the way back home, I made myself available to my team to ask me questions about anything, including leadership development. We stopped off at Starbucks™ so I could treat my staff, and during this time, I allowed them to ask me stuff one-on-one that they didn't want to ask in front of the others. All of these times are important, so you have to make room in your schedule for them.

When you know your team, you can pick out who will ask you questions in front of the crowd and who will hang around until afterward to ask you something they don't want everyone else to hear. As a leader and time manager, I ought to know this about my own staff. So I plan for hang-out time after the meeting's finished, so those people can come and talk to me.

Notice, the schedule just says we went to work on the Christmas event, but we got a bunch of children's ministry stuff done while we were working on that outreach.

When we got back, I worked in the office for a bit: followed up on messages, e-mails, paperwork, and met with my assistant about things she needed to tell me. Then I went and worked out. That day I rode the stationary bike for about an hour and had a chance to read my book in the process. I also talked to four or five people and worked on getting them plugged into children's ministry, so I was working out and recruiting.

After my workout, I called my wife and found out that she was coming to church for our school's basketball games. So I went back to my office to work and write. Then, when my wife called to tell me she was on her way, I asked her to bring me a smoothie for supper, and I packed up. On my way out, I talked to my assistant children's pastor, and then I called my other assistant for Jim Wideman Ministries and checked on Jim Wideman Ministries stuff while my wife was driving to church.

I arrived at the game in time to see the second half of the girls' basketball game and the first half of the boys'. Rather than go to two games and take up all that time, I usually would go to the respective halves and be done early. That way, I could see the kids play and give them my support, plus I had time to talk to the families, kiss the babies, and schmooze with the other church people. Afterward, I walked my wife to the car, and she took me to mine. I called my son-in-law to encourage him some more about starting his own business. And I also called Whitney to check on her. When I got home, I spent some time talking with my family and Whitney's friend. Then I spent some more time writing, checked my e-mail, looked over my calendar to evaluate my day and plan for the next. After I did a little bit more reading, I went to bed.

Always Evaluate

I want you to see that it's really important when looking at your schedule to go back and say, "How could I do that differently? How could I do it better? What needs to be done still?" Looking over those few days, while that wasn't a typical week because of the extra Christmas stuff, it is typical of how many different things that I try to work on at the same time.

When I first started multitasking and evaluating how I was spending time, I noticed that I was not quick at changing hats and working on different departments. That is a skill that I believe only comes from practice. It just takes time to be able to walk through a building and be blindsided with a question about a department you weren't thinking of at that time. To be able to switch gears that quickly took me years to develop. And until that skill was developed in my life, I just blocked my week differently. For example, if Monday was my off day, Tuesday I'd work on nursery stuff, Wednesday was elementary, Thursday was preschool, and Friday was just a day to catch up. Once I could manage well with that schedule, I learned how to jump back and forth between different departments in one day. But don't start out trying to juggle all of your things in one day. Go ahead and assign some days with some routines focused on one project and other days focused on another. Just get in the habit of doing that first.

10

MY LIFE TODAY

Nowadays, since moving from Oklahoma to Tennessee, my life is a lot more structured and full of routine. Starting over in a new place, World Outreach Church, with an already established staff and program has called for me to be deliberate in building relationships and letting people get to know my heart and desire to be a blessing to the vision of this ministry. I am deliberate in making sure that I don't come in and make it like previous churches for my own sake.

My routine has changed quite a bit. For example, my Sundays start earlier than any other day. I don't go to Starbucks™ every day because I can save time by brewing it at home. When I get to the church, like my previous church, I start my rounds, check the building, love on people, and evaluate the strengths and weaknesses of our team. I check in with my pastor who is not in a speaker's room but out among the people as well. I then continue my rounds and sit in as many prayer times as I can. I then take time to love on the teams, kids, and parents until service starts.

Once service has begun, I make announcements and receive the offering in one of our three sanctuaries. Then I attend one service with my family and use the other service to coach, model, and evaluate our children's classrooms and teams. I'm out with the people after each service until I head home for Sunday lunch with my family. Yes, we still keep this tradition with whichever family members are in town. I use the time after lunch to love on family and to rest.

Sundays at 4:00 P.M. is my time for training meetings with large groups of leaders and coordinators. We have Sunday evening services, so I rotate between attending, speaking, and checking on children's ministry programs. We do our baby dedications every other month on Sunday night, and I also use one Sunday night per month to train our college ministry leaders at my home. The rest of the evening is family time and time to watch TV programs we have recorded on the DVR from the previous week.

Monday is a day of revisiting the weekend. We celebrate the God events we see happening before us in the lives of people. We spend the morning writing thank-you notes for children's ministry, and my student ministry teams have a planning and production meeting. I attend a production meeting over lunch where we eat and discuss the hits and misses of the past weekend. We both review and look ahead to the upcoming week so we can make assignments and plans. I use Monday afternoons to go over my staff's weekly reports, and I plan the staff meetings and agendas for Tuesday. I use Mondays for phone appointments and one-on-one appointments with individuals and families concerning their pursuit of God. Then I leave to do cardio before I have to be back for our college ministry small groups. My wife and Whitney help me with this ministry, so we get to minister as a family. After college ministry, Julie goes to bed; I stay up checking the Internet and working on Infuse stuff (see www.jimwideman.com for more information).

Tuesday is a day of meetings. Since I'm at the church late Monday night, I come in late Tuesday morning. I check in with my assistant before heading to our all-church staff meeting. The meeting always starts with reports about what God is doing before us, and then it moves to a time of going over the calendar, training or vision casting, teaching a skill set, or a combination of all of the above. It rarely last more than an hour—one of my favorite parts of working at World Outreach Church. After the staff meeting, I prepare for my afternoon meetings, return calls, and check e-mails. I also try to have lunch with as many of my children's ministry staff as will go. Then I'm back for a 1:30 P.M. meeting with either my children's ministry staff or my student ministry staff. (I rotate so they only meet every other week while my assistant and I attend them all.) I use the time after the meeting to get with staff individuals as needed based on their weekly reports. I leave the office around 3:30 P.M. and head to work out with my personal trainer and do cardio. Tuesday nights I reserve for family or Infuse calls.

Wednesday is one of my favorite days because it's just so much more laid back than the other days. Wednesday seems to be my day to get my work done. I have a standing executive team meeting at 10:00 A.M. Then I also have a standing lunch with my student ministry staff. Wednesday afternoon is filled with working on what I need to work on. Wednesday nights I rotate checking on children's ministry folks and our middle school ministry.

Thursday starts with another production meeting to make sure we are ready for the weekend services. We view any video piece or anything at all that will affect the weekend services. This meeting lasts thirty minutes at the longest, but it's a great way to eliminate surprises from the weekend. Afterward, I have a weekly meeting with my pastor. We use this time not only to discuss our next-generation ministries but also as a time for my pastor and I to get to know one another and work on our relationship.

My Thursday lunches are reserved for key volunteers. The rest of the day is my time to love on people, put into leadership, phone appointments, one-on-one meetings, and to help my staff prepare for the weekend. Just like Tuesday, I work out with my personal trainer and do cardio. My Thursday nights I rotate with Wednesday. If I didn't attend Wednesday night's service, I attend Thursday night's high school service at least once a month. The Thursdays I don't attend senior high, I do a conference call with one of my Infuse groups.

Friday is my day off and my only day that I can deliberately sleep in. It's really Julie's day because we start with a bike ride or just time together and keep it up all day long. We try to have lunch together and keep it a fun day for us. Friday night is date night for us. One of the things we love about living near family and Nashville is that we can check on my mom sometimes on Fridays. We can also take in one of the many concerts that come through Music City. Saturday mornings are some of my favorite study times, writing times, and Jim Wideman Ministries times. Because of the craziness of my daughters' schedules, our Saturday lunches have turned into Saturday breakfasts.

Before I know it, it's time to start getting ready for weekend church again. Our first weekend services get going on Saturday evening, so I do on Saturdays what I also do on Sundays; starting my rounds an hour before the first service starts, and then repeating at 7:00 P.M. what I did at 5:00 P.M. After the second service is over, I head home to see who's still up to love on. I use Saturday nights to have a little me-time with a concert DVD, sports broadcasts, or playing guitar for a bit in my man wing. Then it's off to bed getting ready for the best day of the week, Sunday.

I am so thankful that I learned the principles that I have written in this book. They are not just what I have *learned*, they are what I *live*. I lean on these principles today more than ever. You can have time for whatever you want too! You can get it all done and have time left over.

Meet Jim Wideman_____

Jim Wideman is an internationally recognized voice in children's and family ministry. He is a much sought after speaker, teacher, author, personal leadership coach, and ministry consultant who has over 30 years experience in helping churches thrive.

Having served in 5 dynamic churches, Jim understands what it takes to grow exciting, relevant ministries to people of all ages. For 17 years Jim led one of America's largest local church children's ministries in Tulsa, OK. Jim has also held various other positions in addition to children ministry throughout his career giving him a background in almost every area of the local church and Christian school. Jim currently serves as Associate Pastor at World Outreach Church in Murfreesboro, TN where he oversees the next generation and family ministries.

In addition to working in a local church, Jim has successfully trained hundreds of thousands of children's ministry leaders from all denominations and sizes of congregations in conferences and seminars around the world. Jim is considered an innovator, pioneer and father in the modern children's ministry movement. He also currently serves as president of "The American Children's Ministry Association," as well as president of Jim Wideman Ministries and is one of the executive editors of K! Magazine. The International Network of Children's Pastors awarded Jim the "Excellence in Ministry Award" in 1989 for his outstanding work in Children's Ministry, and Children's Ministry Magazine in 2001 honored him as one of ten "Pioneers of the Decade" in children's ministry.

Jim created the Children's Ministers Leadership Club in 1995 that is known today as "theClub" which has touched thousands of ministry leaders each month. This monthly audio leadership resource is still impacting leaders and causing them to think differently and become better leaders now! In 2007, Jim introduced a personal mentorship program called infuse where he, and a hand-picked group of leaders, coach and mentor 20 leaders for a year. (A new group of 20 start every six months).

Jim has one burning desire and that is to help others become better leaders. Jim believes his matching orders are to spend the rest of his life taking what he has learned about leadership and ministry and pour it into the next generation of children's, youth, and family ministry leaders.

For more information go to www.jimwideman.com

What others are saying about Jim…

> *"I have watched Jim Wideman for a number of years. You can trust his heart and his counsel as a leader who has a passion to see churches succeed in reaching the next generation. His experience at helping churches navigate through change and develop problem solving techniques makes him a valuable asset to any church or ministry. Jim has the mind of an administrator, the heart of a pastor, the wit of a comedian, and the soul of a musician. I always know when I'm on my way to spend time with Jim, I am going to walk away warmed, motivated, entertained and equipped to be a better leader and thinker."*
> – **Reggie Joiner,** Re-Think Group

> *"Jim is a walking encyclopedia of information concerning ministry and management in the local church. Best known for his unique ability to recruit, train, and retain both employees and volunteers, Jim is a highly creative individual who meets challenges head-on. As one of America's top leaders in the area of children's ministry, his knowledge of daily operations in the local church is*

unmatched. I strongly recommend Jim Wideman as both a consultant and seminar instructor."

– Joe McGee,
Joe McGee Ministries// Tulsa, OK

"I always watch for the leader who can lead us through the challenges of our complicated world and Jim Wideman is one of those unique men. He can lead without compromising the integrity of the mission. Excellence and value are obvious expressions when describing the leadership of Jim Wideman. Personally, I have known him for over 20 years and have admired his creativity as a gifted thinker and communicator. Some people talk about doing it. Jim has done it. I highly recommend Jim Wideman for whatever creative venue you are wanting to advance to the next level."

– Steve Dixon, Senior Pastor, Christian Life Cathedral // Fayetteville, AR

Other books from jimwideman.com_____

Children's Ministry In The 21st Century

Volunteers That Stick

Children's Ministry Leadership-the you can do it guide

Children's Ministry That Works

Connect With Your Kids

Turning Your Child's Failures Into Success

Breinigsville, PA USA
16 June 2010
240029BV00003B/1/P